Victoria Cosford

Amore
and
Amaretti

A tale of love and food in Italy

McArthur & Company
Toronto

First published in Canada in 2011 by
McArthur & Company
322 King Street West, Suite 402
Toronto, Ontario
M5V 1J2
www.mcarthur-co.com

First Australian edition published in 2010 by Wakefield Press.
First UK edition published in 2010 by Summersdale.
This Canadian edition published by arrangement with Wakefield Press.

Library and Archives Canada Cataloguing in Publication

Cosford, Victoria
        Amore and amaretti : a tale of love and food in Italy / Victoria
Cosford.

Includes index.
ISBN 978-1-55278-943-8

        1. Cosford, Victoria--Travel--Italy--Tuscany. 2. Gastronomy--
Italy--Tuscany. 3. Tuscany (Italy)--Biography. 4. Tuscany (Italy)--
Description and travel. I. Title.

DG734.23.C68 2011   914.5'50493   C2010-907603-6

Cover design by Debbie Clement
Printed in Canada by Webcom

10 9 8 7 6 5 4 3 2 1

Amore
and
Amaretti

A tale of love and food in Italy

To my two sisters, whose unbounded
faith in me never once wavered

Contents

ITALY

Abetone

Venice

Florence

Strada-in-Chianti

Rimini

San Casciano

Greve

Riccione

Isle of Elba
Portoferraio

Siena

Perugia

Rome

Prelude

I might be walking along a street when I hear it. Unmistakable Italian words, a sentence, a conversation, uttered in that musical poetry so immediately familiar that I am shocked out of my previous self-absorption and swallowed into the sensuousness of the sound.

Yet, here I am in Australia, in another hemisphere, where I rarely give a serious thought to Italy, the country that changed my life and indirectly brought me to the place where I am today. I am living in Byron Bay, writing about food in a weekly column, reporting on general news stories for the local newspaper and occasionally teaching Italian cooking.

Someone famous – was it Virginia Woolf? – once said, 'Do the hardest thing.' It seems to me that my time spent in Italy was precisely that and it has brought me circuitously to contentment and the reward of true love.

Book One

1982–1986
Florence, Isle of Elba, Perugia

Quando si ama, anche i sassi diventono stelle
When you're in love, even pebbles become stars

One Florentine Friday night, a man with a tea towel tossed over one shoulder unclasps his watch and places it at the end of the table I share with twenty international students. This is how it begins, in a restaurant in a cellar. We belong to the Michelangelo Institute, where we are studying the language and culture of Italy; every Friday night we unwind over dinner in a typical Tuscan trattoria.

When I think about the small incidental objects that had the power to transform my life, I always return to that watch. Over the years, it became magnified in my mind, effulgent with significance. Its territorial presence on the table of *his* restaurant means that Gianfranco can come and go with ease, with a sort of claim on the two foreign women it lies closest to, my sister and me. Toward the end of the evening, there he is sitting with us, conversing in a clumsy cocktail of languages over wine.

Gianfranco is a country boy from a village in Umbria whose Italian is loose, lazy and colloquial, whose French is meagre though elegant, whose Dutch, owing to a ten-month-long marriage to a Dutch woman, is fluent,

14

but whose English is sparse. We understand each other magnificently.

He smokes Marlboros and wears expensive gold jewellery and tight jeans; there is a swaggish indifference to him to which I am drawn, so that by the end of the night, when somehow we have ended up at a bar at Piazzale Michelangelo, I am already a little in love. He is dancing on the mirrored floor with my sister and I am dancing with Roberto, the apprentice chef, who is asking me to translate into Italian the words of a Chicago song, which I do badly. Gianfranco brings me a glass of Cointreau with ice in it, and we sit down together with our knees touching. Roberto and my sister seem to melt away.

I had been in Italy for several weeks. I had already fallen in love with the country, the people, Florence, the director of the Institute. A degree in languages at university had led me indirectly here via jobs in advertising and nursing, a lonely year in London growing fat as a live-in barmaid, and the breakup of a relationship, grown too cosy, too lazy, with a gentle man named Tony whom I no longer loved.

Tony had arrived in London before me and met me at the airport, as arranged. In our six months apart, while he did the overland Magic Bus trip and I saved up, I had already changed, so that when I put my arms around his cheap new leather coat I felt that I was embracing a brother, not a lover. His decision to return to Australia was met with relief on my part; my adventurous life had only just begun. I found a job at the Museum Tavern opposite the British Museum and moved into a small room upstairs, where I worked my way through *War and Peace* on evenings off after solitary excursions to other pubs to sit over glasses of South African wine and dry-roasted peanuts.

My younger sister had flown from Australia to join me in Italy and the Institute had organised rooms for us in a boarding house near the Duomo that we shared with Scandinavian girls enrolled in the same course. London was already seeping out of me. I had begun to sling jumpers casually around my shoulders, the way Italian girls did, and knot scarves loosely around my white Anglo-Saxon throat... And, now, there is Gianfranco.

Gianfranco picks me up from the boarding house near the Duomo for our first official date. He has parked illegally, and our awkwardness is overshadowed by our haste to flee the city centre, like criminals in a stolen car, and by the time we are driving through outer suburbs I am almost relaxed. Our stop-start conversation is punctured by my tedious admissions of not understanding and carries us all the way to an unremarkable hotel on the town's edge. Gianfranco parks the car and bustles me inside in a proprietary way I find both arousing and significant, then orders food from a waiter he clearly knows well. Earlier nervousness has narrowed my appetite to a thread but I do my best to try a little of everything: sliced meats and pickled vegetables, a winey stew on steaming gold polenta, little red capsicums stuffed with rice and herbs. We drink wine, which later allows me to float up the flight of stairs to an impersonal room with little more than a bed and a television set, where I am undressed by Gianfranco, the blinds lowered. A fleeting sense that I have been too easily won is displaced by the great and glorious joy of our coming together, a feeling that I have disappeared inside his body.

But still I am unconvinced he really likes me. I console myself by concentrating on his less appealing qualities: he is brash, but I close my eyes to a mouth of chipped and neglected teeth in my determination not to be superficial. I have been told about his reputation with foreign women, but cannot believe he actually finds me attractive. It is easier, in those cautious early days, to persuade myself that I am using him as much as he is using me, to be the hard, bright woman I really am not. But in truth I am always in Gianfranco's power; he has the advantage of being himself on his own terrain, master of the language, while I struggle, apologising and requesting enlightenment.

As it turns out I have nothing to worry about. Miraculously – quite magically, it seems to me – Gianfranco begins to betray the fact he is as enraptured by me as I am by him. When I have established that *'ti voglio bene'* means 'I love you', and I hear him tell me often, I begin to shyly say it back.

I study my lover. His cheeks point outward when he smiles. He roars his welcome to customers and friends; rooms feel empty when he leaves them. He moves quickly, heels clicking across the uneven stones of his restaurant and while crossing roads. He has friends everywhere: fashionable glittery Florentines whom he intimately addresses as *dottore*, plumbers and carpenters and shopkeepers, and a vast repertoire of waiters and cooks with whom he has worked. His profession is chef, but he is better suited to front of house with his boyish boisterousness and his easy charm.

I have never met anyone like Gianfranco before, a man so sure of his place in the world. He whistles loudly, in perfect pitch, and dispenses with the endings of names, so that after a while I become simply 'Vee'. I marvel in those early days at the miracle of having found him, at being swept up into the orb of his volatility and spontaneity, driven to edge-of-town hotels for the night, taken to country restaurants and to the seaside.

I am not spending the amount of time with my sister that I had expected. The late, sleepless nights also mean that I am missing classes at the Institute – but I am beyond caring. The language and culture of Italy are filtering through, regardless.

Gianfranco sweeps me into small shops up side streets, where after good-humoured haggling he hands me a beautiful suede coat with a fur-lined hood wrapped in tissue paper, or a leather skirt, or gold jewellery. He never pays full price for anything; his audacity is breathtaking. We emerge into the sunlight, holding hands, each with new reversible leather belts. He is funny, smart, generous beyond measure – this is all I see in those early days. I am gradually substituting the cool stone rooms of his restaurant for those of the Institute, until one day I simply stop attending the course. Most lunchtimes I sit in the front room of the restaurant typing out the daily menu with one finger, spellbound by the names of the different Chiantis recommended each day: Geografico and Capezzano, Grignanello and Castello di Volpaia, Lamole di Lamole and Villa La Pagliaia. Then I move inside to the warmth of the dining room to sit beside my beloved and pick disinterestedly at the titbits he places before me.

Evenings I am back, perfumed and party-ish, to sit and sit and sit, drinking too much, writing love poems on the recycled paper placemats which double as menus before reeling off into the late night on Gianfranco's arm. Gianfranco drives his blue Fiat very fast up the narrow snaking streets to Fiesole with Deep Purple thundering out the open window. One time, with my sister in the back, I turn around to say that it wouldn't matter if I died at that moment, I am so brimming with happiness, and when she agrees we look at each other a little shocked.

No longer students at the Michelangelo Institute, my sister and I are obliged to look for accommodation elsewhere. We move from the boarding house and, thanks to an advertisement in the free weekly *Il Pulce*, into an apartment in an unfamiliar suburb away from the heart of the city, sharing with Anna and Franco. Initially we adore this unconventional couple; they strike us as modern and un-Italian. Anna is tall with a long plait of black hair that reaches to the waist of her billowy Indian dresses; Franco, a stub of a man, has his long hair tied back in a ponytail. Posters on the apartment walls depict peace marches and alternative lifestyles. Remnants of the 1960s, they have a little art-and-craft shop nearby, filled with mostly dust-covered junk and generally devoid of customers. The evenings when my sister and I have not caught the bus into the Santa Maria Novella Piazza to descend stairs to Salt Peanuts, our favourite underground jazz cellar, we sit at the long table in our room drinking Chianti and eating bread and cheese with the door firmly closed.

Increasingly, inexplicably, Anna becomes stranger and stranger. Sometimes she will ignore us when we address her, or say something cold and vituperative we cannot properly understand. The one night I dare to have Gianfranco stay, she storms into our room and commences shrieking at the top of her voice about wet towels lying on the bathroom floor and how she cannot take it any more; humiliated, Gianfranco slinks away. We are left uncomprehending and open-mouthed, having believed we had been respectful, polite, cheerful guests in their home, and concluding that Anna is simply mad. We start to look for another place.

I ask Gianfranco, in my slowly improving Italian, how he can be so patient with my limited grasp of his language and his world. This is well before his displays of spectacular tantrums – all I see are deep-brown eyes of unwavering kindness as I labour to articulate my feelings and navigate conversations. He tells me that it is only with me that he manages to be patient.

One lunchtime I step down into the coolness of his restaurant and find Gianfranco sitting in front of a box of figs. Before he looks up, I see that what he is doing with a small sharp knife, his forehead knotted in concentration, is carefully peeling fig after fig and setting them aside. He resembles a little boy whittling wood, and when he presents me with the plate of peeled figs my stomach twists with love.

Il pasto non vale un'acca se alla fine non s' ha la vacca
The meal means nothing if it does not end in good cheese

My understanding of Italian food begins to take shape in Gianfranco's Umbrian village. Most Sunday nights, after the benches are stacked on top of tables and the floor mopped at his restaurant, we set off on our midnight journey; tomorrow is our day off. Two hours out of Florence, passing glassy, spectral Lake Trasimeno, the hill towns of Tuscany are replaced by the hill towns of medieval Umbria. Gianfranco races all the bends, fuelled by Chianti, not bothering with seatbelts, belting out Battiato songs. I sit cross-legged beside him, tired eyes mesmerised by points of light in the rushing blackness. His village in my mind always seems to be arising out of the mist, its few streets coiling past low doorways and bars, the butcher shop with a burning cigarette resting on the chopping block. And yet most of my time there is spent at the service station and its accompanying bar, both run by Gianfranco's sister.

We pull into the heavy silence of the sleeping village; Bar Due Raspi – Two Bunches – glows dimly, warmly.

Gianfranco's sister raises two children, husbandless, in the attached house, assisted by Mamma. In the kitchen little feasts are left for us under cloths: a round of aged pecorino, a hunk of prosciutto, hard-boiled eggs and spicy salami, plump new broad beans and a dome of cheese bread. Gianfranco splashes rough red wine into tumblers and carves off chunks of cheese and passes me salami slices speared on the tip of his pocket knife. I feel like a rosy-cheeked maiden from another century, in the absolute stillness of a country village, with a man I am not terribly sure I know – but whom I feel terribly sure I love – who is offering me the great gift of this experience. I seem to exist solely for him, and in our whispered conversation and the simplicity of the setting there seems to be the possibility for more joy than I ever considered possible.

And of course there are the lunches. On Sundays we only work the evening shift, so at midday we often drive to share a meal with friends. I had never cared about lunch, until I was introduced to Sunday ones in Tuscan vineyards. Celebrations of food and wine amongst friends and family, they transcend the notion of mere meals and transform into a theatre for the senses.

It has much to do with the setting, the compelling beauty of ancient surroundings, of land which has yielded produce for millennia, of eroded stone walls and roads which wind through hills, and row upon row upon row of vines. There is little more glorious, in summer, than sitting through hours of golden afternoons at a long wooden table with twelve or sixteen or twenty others, in winter warming limbs and souls with fires and food and wine.

Gianfranco has friends at Montespertoli and we go there often, mostly for winter lunches. We crunch up the circular gravel driveway and arrive at the back door, which leads into a vast stone kitchen filled with people. The ancient stove roars with flames, heating an assortment of saucepans, which steam forth wonderful aromas. Someone is carving a prosciutto, Claret-red slices sliding off the edge of the knife. There are women to stir the saucepans, wash the salad, slice the bread. I make myself useful by carrying cutlery to the dining room, where men pose around the leaping fire, clutching glasses of Campari and smoking. Hand-painted jugs of water and flowers clutter the table. I set for eighteen people, folding paper napkins into tiny triangles beside each plate. Two-litre bottles of home-grown Chianti, translucent red, line up like soldiers. Outside the tall windows, mist wraps around bare trees and church spires.

Platters are placed on the table: slices of wild-boar salami, tiny spicy venison sausages, rounds of toast topped with coarse chicken-liver pâté sweetened with Marsala, shiny black olives tossed in garlic and parsley. Wine is tipped into glasses and wedges of crusty spongy bread are passed around. Lunch has begun.

Pasta comes next, a deep ceramic bowl of steaming spaghetti in a simple tomato sauce fragrant with fresh basil, or a rich cream redolent of wild mushrooms. On top of the fire have been placed two metal grills, which clip together to enclose the main course: thick slabs of prime beef, a handful of quails, fat home-made sausages. Passed around the table they are black-striped and crisp from the flames, perfumed with fresh rosemary, garlic and good oil.

Afterwards there is a chunk of Parmesan, aged and crumbly, and a tangy pecorino from Sardinia to eat with a large bowl of various fruits. This is the winding-down stage of the lunch, when women begin to push back chairs and carry out plates and men light up cigarettes and pour whisky. Coffee brews aromatic from the kitchen, conversation subdues, becomes sleepy, comfortable and confidential. Pastries accompany the coffee: a wealth of shortbreads, crunchy almond biscuits, macaroons and iced eclairs bulging cream. Vin Santo, sweet and dark, is poured into small glasses; outside the evening has begun to descend, and Sunday lunch settles.

Whereas at Montespertoli the high stone walls surround the house like a stronghold, and the sense of place comes only once you have passed the gates and commenced the descent down winding roads that curve through the fields of grapes and olives, Claudia and Vincenzo Sabatini's villa sits on top of a hill, and looking down from the verandah you can see the vineyards stretch for miles. Even in winter clustered around their smaller hearth, warming hands, we always have the windows throwing up vistas of rich land, visions of space and ordered growth.

And in summer it is all there below. Slow yellow afternoons pulse with warmth and the tiny incessant rhythms of a million twitching insects. The verandah has canvas drapes to shut out the sun, and the table is cool. As we arrive we are handed a glass of Vincenzo's wine – not of his making but wine he collects weekly in huge vats from the villa next door, which he decants and stores in his cellar. Claudia is tasting the pasta sauce for salt: she looks harassed but happy, hair escaping from her bun and her apron spattered with flour. She has been making *pappardelle*, wide uneven strips of pasta that will be served with hare sauce. Vincenzo, having dispensed wine to his guests, is washing lettuces from his garden then drying them in his salad-spinner. Our movements are languid. We eat home-grown egg tomatoes drizzled with green olive oil and fresh basil, thick slices of moist white mozzarella, paper-thin cuts of cured beef dressed with oil, finely chopped rocket leaves and shavings of Parmesan cheese, mushrooms marinated in lemon juice and garlic, strips of red and green capsicum bathed in oil, garlic and parsley, slices of spicy pancetta. There is crusty bread to mop up the juices, and Vincenzo's wine is flowing freely. Next comes Claudia's pasta, rich and gamey. Then a pause before she brings out a casserole of pheasant scented with red wine and herbs. There is silverbeet sautéed in garlic, and tiny chunks of potatoes oven-roasted with rosemary and rock salt, and Vincenzo's salad gleaming with oil. Afterwards comes a whole fresh ricotta cheese, and ripe pears.

Much later, in the fading day, with the beginnings of breezes lifting leaves and stirring the air, Claudia brings out coffee and her famous biscuits, which it is never possible to eat in moderation, whose secret recipe she has given me and which I have lost. Cicadas start up their buzzing hum, and the vineyards lie pale and ghostly in the moonlight. I am drowsy, aware of the desire to freeze time so I can always remain in this comfortable chair, breathing in the fragrant evening air, all senses gratified.

Gianfranco buys another restaurant with several partners. It is in the centre of Florence, with the Uffizi and a replica of David around the corner. I am in the enormous kitchen wearing an apron, being shown how to finely chop onions; how to make a basic tomato sauce; how to flick my right wrist so that the contents of a frying pan flip briefly in the air; how to cook pasta, separating the strands of spaghetti with a giant fork and knowing the exact moment when to drain it, just a touch ahead of al dente – firm to the bite – so the extra minute or so of tossing it in its hot sauce will render it perfect. I learn how to make *crespelle* – paper-thin crêpes – and béchamel, soups and slowly simmering stews, panna cotta without gelatine; and I learn the elaborate process of layering that goes into creating pasta sauces, like the *salsa puttanesca*.

Gianfranco becomes less patient and more critical, however. There are days when I can do nothing right. I see the flipside of his creativity, a sort of madness. Saucepans fly, crashing into walls. An hour later, he is carving a rose out of a radish, his face gentle and his fingers graceful. For a country boy, those fingers are strangely delicate, almost feminine – each night he scrubs his nails vigorously with Jif.

Six months later, I am running the kitchen of the restaurant while Gianfranco escorts customers to tables. And we are living together, having moved into a flat nearby. I have

Spaghetti alla puttanesca

Olive oil
1 medium onion
3 cloves garlic
4–6 slices pancetta
Dried chilli (optional)
2 tablespoons black olives
5 anchovies
1 tablespoon capers
1/3 cup red wine
400 g peeled tomatoes
Salt and pepper
Chopped parsley

Heat the oil, then add finely chopped onion and garlic
together with sliced pancetta and chilli, if desired. Sauté 5 to 8
minutes on medium heat, stirring frequently, until translucent.
Throw in olives. Cook several more minutes, then add finely
chopped anchovies and capers. After several more minutes,
slosh in wine. Bring to the boil and bubble until evaporated,
then add peeled tomatoes and about half a cup of water.
Season cautiously with salt and pepper, bring back to the
boil, then simmer 30 to 40 minutes. Garnish with parsley.

grown thin with the long, unforgiving hours of work, but mostly with love and anxiety.

One summer midnight I am the only woman in a carload of murmuring men. We park near the river not far from Gianfranco's village and I watch as torches thread through the darkness and down to the edge, where bottles of bleach are poured into the water. Downstream, more torch lights illumine men wading with plastic bags, into which they throw the dead trout. I am appalled, disillusioned, excited and terrified all at the same time.

The next day, a long table is set under trees at lunchtime. There are dishes full of steaming potato gnocchi with rabbit sauce, and platters of trout simply grilled. Everyone eats the sweet pink fish; nobody becomes ill. Glasses are raised to the fishermen.

Other times we go hunting for mushrooms. Autumn is the season for porcini – these treasures lurk around the base of chestnut trees and oaks. Often the size of dinner plates, they are as fleshy as meat. Many *trattorie* place baskets of porcini at the entrance, and, like lobsters at Chinese restaurants, they are selected by the customer, weighed, cooked and served. Studded with slivers of garlic, brushed with good olive oil and grilled is the best way to enjoy these musky, musty gifts from the forest floor, with their flavour of faintly sweetish decay.

On these mushroom expeditions I am fascinated by delicate, beautiful specimens in iridescent colours, which Gianfranco warns me are deadly. I dare not even stand too close, lest the air is contaminated by their garish toxicity.

Salsa di coniglio
(Rabbit sauce)

Olive oil
Bay leaf
1 rabbit, jointed*
1 medium onion, finely chopped
2 sticks celery, finely chopped
1 carrot, finely chopped
3 cloves garlic, finely chopped
1/2 cup white wine
400 g peeled tomatoes
Salt and pepper
Dried chilli (optional)

Heat olive oil in low, wide pan and add bay leaf and rabbit.
Brown rabbit pieces all over, season, then remove and set
aside. In the same pan sauté onion, celery, carrot and garlic
until softened, about 8 to 10 minutes. Return rabbit to pan.
Slosh in white wine and let it bubble up and evaporate before
adding peeled tomatoes, about 1/2 cup water and chilli if
desired. Season again, bring to the boil, then simmer about 40
minutes for farmed rabbit and 2 hours if wild, topping up with
water when sauce reduces too much. Check seasoning. When
cool, remove rabbit meat from bones, then return to sauce,
reheating at least 5 minutes before tossing through pasta.

* If using wild rabbit, soak it overnight in water or
wine and herbs to remove some of its 'gaminess'.

We pick, pluck and gather and, because he is a country boy, we have no need to carry our collection into the nearest *farmacia*, where they would readily identify the various types for us. We dine on massive porcini, with lots of bread for the luscious juices.

Several months into my Florentine life, life with Gianfranco, I hear about permanent contact lenses. Lavish advertisements depict their miraculous powers: lenses you can keep in for days at a time, lenses you can sleep in, lenses that will change your life. Having been desperately short-sighted since my teens, as I juggled glasses with contact lenses I must remove every night, I am naturally intrigued, then seduced. And despite their tremendous cost – but then what value can be placed on a miracle? – Gianfranco is marching me briskly into Pisacchi the optometrist.

I submit to the sort of eye examination I have had regularly since I was thirteen, and the optometrist speaks slowly and carefully to make sure I understand. My two years of university Italian, combined with the six weeks or so at the Michelangelo Institute, all reinforced by the past months in which Italian is what I mostly hear and speak (if not perfectly understand), have made me a little reckless, even cocky in my confidence. '*Si, capisco*' – Yes, I understand – I say. We pay for my exciting new lenses with half my month's salary and then speed off to Viareggio to spend what remains of our day at the beach. The world seems brimming with possibilities that the past decade and a half of myopia had closed to me. As we drive, Gianfranco is telling me how Italy has long been at the forefront of optical technologies, pioneering techniques and equipment.

We arrive at the beach in blazing sunshine, change into swimming attire and hurl ourselves into the water. I am so accustomed to keeping my eyes fiercely shut under water that it has become instinct. And yet the optometrist had spoken so enthusiastically about *'il fare la doccia'* – having a shower – or *'un bagno'* – a bath, or bathing – that the next time I go under I stare wide-eyed and defiant into the glassy curl of wave.

In that moment a strange sensation takes place as the sharp clarity of my vision gives way to a soft and familiar blur. The expensive lenses have floated out of my eyes, lost in the infinite expanse of ocean, possibly even drifting towards Australia. I can hardly believe it has happened, that I possessed those permanent lenses so temporarily. It is only afterwards, when I confess to Gianfranco what has happened, that the optometrist's directions are revealed to me. The only thing you *cannot* do, Gianfranco smiles as he reports what had apparently been said in one of those sentences I pretended to understand, is to open your eyes under water.

The Fiat is slipping through drifts of snow and navigating treacherous bends to bring our carload of friends, unharmed, to Pettino. A lone farmhouse glows amber, welcoming us in. We are the only guests tonight at this trattoria, where the family, clustering around the fireplace, springs into attendance. The dining room is merely long wooden tables and wooden benches. The ambience soon softens around the curl of cigarette smoke, the uncorking of wine bottles and our shrill exuberance at having risked such roads in such conditions. There is no menu; we have come to eat truffles. I have heard about the nonchalance with which Umbrians treat this precious ingredient, like parsley or potatoes. Instead of being finely grated or shaved, they are often cut into chunks.

First arrives the crostini, crisp little toasts piled with a mixture of anchovies and finely chopped mushrooms specked with black truffles. There is a frittata perfumed with pecorino and truffles. Eggy threads of fresh tagliatelle arrive truffle-flecked and glistening with green oil. Everything else – the snow outside, the members of the family coming and going, the sharp wooden contours of the austere room – becomes a fuzzy frame for our truffle tasting. We stay for hours and the euphoria carries us all the way, dangerously back, cosy beyond caring.

Wherever we end up – at the midnight end of busy restaurant days, on our precious one day off, during an impromptu arrival of friends, in Florence or out – our meals are always memorable. Gianfranco possesses the happy combination of both peasant background and swish Swiss hospitality training, so I am mostly happy to let him do the choosing. He knows about food; his palate is impeccable. The other sides I begin to see of him – the moody volatility, the surly suspiciousness – are often with us now, like unwanted guests at a feast, faceless and brooding. He has begun to ignore me inexplicably and we live in the thick walls of my love's jealous silences. Later, when his mood has recovered, he justifies it on the grounds of jealousy towards someone like the corner greengrocer whose name I do not even know. And yet, when I watch his skill at mealtimes, my admiration for him enables easy forgiveness.

We invariably eat whatever is seasonal, freshest, *del giorno*, and a little unusual. He heads immediately for the kitchen of whatever establishment we are visiting, where through the servery windows I watch him dip fingers into steamy cauldrons. All the places we frequent are staffed by waiters or chefs whom he knows, or with whom he has worked. Their stories are told to me over crisp-crusted pizza with curls of prosciutto on top, and are continued through the last lemon vodkas of the night. How Tonino squandered a family inheritance on gambling and is now forced to work three jobs; why one of Silvio's legs is shorter than the other; where Paolo takes his mistress to dine on the nights he is able to escape his overbearing, cruel wife.

Massive Claudio's pizzeria in Piazza Santa Croce is one of our favourites. I love best his spinach sautéed quickly in garlic, chilli and olive oil, which I eat with too much bread, while all around me waiters knock off for the night to play cards, smoke and drink with up-rolled sleeves.

We eat often at the elegant Antica Toscana, which specialises in tour groups and is owned by a gravel-voiced man called Lorenzo, one of Gianfranco's partners. I warm to Lorenzo immediately, to the fact that he is not only urbane but clearly a devoted family man who takes great pride in the two sons who are often there helping out. It is here that I meet a multilingual, accordion-playing, walrus-moustachioed waiter called Raimondo, who is to become a great friend. We pull

Spinaci con olio, aglio e peperoncino
(Spinach with oil, garlic and chilli)

Wash and squeeze-dry a bunch of spinach. Heat olive oil in a pan and add garlic slivers and dried chilli, then the spinach. Season with salt and pepper, then toss for several minutes. Serve with a squeeze of fresh lemon juice and a generous slick of extra virgin olive oil.

up at service stations along the *autostrada*, where in sparse, near-empty dining rooms Gianfranco knows to order soupy stews of intestinal organs, salt cod with silverbeet, wide ribbons of pasta glistening with duck sauce, fresh figs draped with pancetta, a log of creamy tomino bathing in golden oil. In summer, we drive 110 kilometres to the seaside town of Viareggio one evening just to eat fish. In an art deco building on the promenade we are served, naturally, by ex-colleagues of Gianfranco, a banquet of endless platters piled high with seafood stirred through spaghetti or chunked into risotto, or simply gloriously grilled. Sometimes we choose the traditional Tuscan *baccalà*, peasant food now fashionable again.

Gianfranco's ancient mother shuffles through the service station, a tiny figure dressed in black, moustachioed, hair bandaged in a scarf. I find her toothless, colloquial Italian incomprehensible, yet we smile at each other constantly, shyly. She prepares all the meals, her fingers pressing breadcrumbs onto veal cutlets, podding beans and twisting tubes of spinach-stuffed pastry into snakes. Her broad practical hands show me how to iron and fold Gianfranco's white work T-shirts. (I iron them quickly and badly, humiliated by this servile role.) When all the dishes have been brought out to the dining room and the extended family – which now includes '*la Veeky*', the earnest *Australiana* – is noisily jostling with platters, Mamma slips back into the kitchen, where she eats on a chair by the stove.

I love her food and the way it always ends up a feast. I love the way she rolls taut ripe tomatoes onto the table, and

Baccala alla Fiorentina
(Florentine salt cod)

2 leeks
Olive oil
3 cloves garlic
400 g peeled tomatoes
Salt and pepper
800 g salt cod, soaked overnight in several changes of water
Flour
Sprig rosemary

To serve
1 tablespoon chopped parsley
Polenta

For the tomato sauce, clean and finely slice leeks, then soften in olive oil together with 2 cloves of whole, peeled garlic. When the leeks are beginning to colour, add the tomatoes, season with salt and pepper and simmer for 30 to 40 minutes, adding extra water as required. Meanwhile, wash and drain the salt cod well and cut into large pieces. Flour and fry both sides in hot olive oil, to which you have added rosemary and 1 clove garlic. Drain on paper towels and, when the sauce is ready, lay salt cod on top in a single layer. Leave to simmer on low heat for 5 minutes. Check seasoning and serve sprinkled with finely chopped parsley on a bed of polenta.

carves the bread, resting the loaf on her chest – one sharp cut, with her weathered finger pressing down on the blade of the utility knife. She salts everything lavishly, and throws nothing away. Her basic tomato sauce floods the kitchen with a rich sweet perfume as her small sturdy hands prod, test and stir the disintegrating fruit.

I love the way she looks at Gianfranco, her youngest boy, made good in the city, with his high-heeled boots and his jewellery and his bewildering foreign girlfriends. I am frustrated by my inability to express this love, and so I carry plates out to the kitchen, and smile and smile.

Then there is the world of the restaurant, where sixty hours of my week are spent. We are a *birreria-ristorante*, which means there is an enormous selection of local and imported beers available to accompany the meals. Our menu is eclectic and international, thereby ensuring that we are popular with both the fashionable young Florentines who arrive clutching their car radios (to prevent the incessant thefts) and the busloads of tourists; we have something to please all palates. There are the traditional Tuscan offerings – the pastas (including my favourite, the nutmeggy, creamy spinach and ricotta) and Florentine (porterhouse) steaks and anchovy sauces and *crespelle* – alongside a range of hamburgers, pronounced 'umborgers', to go with the beers, and mayonnaise for the French fries. Gianfranco has negotiated special deals for the tourists via a travel agency, and I am often struck by the beautiful irony, as I ladle lemon sauce over 140 veal *scaloppine* before sending them out of the kitchen on platters, that groups of Australian tourists are

Pomarola
(Basic tomato sauce)

Olive oil
1 medium red onion, finely chopped
2–3 cloves garlic, finely sliced
400 g peeled and coarsely chopped tomatoes, tinned or fresh
Salt and pepper

Heat olive oil in saucepan, and add onion and garlic. Stirring frequently, cook about 8 minutes or until softened. Topple in the peeled tomatoes and about 1/2 cup of water. Season with salt and pepper and bring to the boil. Lower heat and simmer 30 to 40 minutes, adding extra water if it reduces too much.

heartily tucking into a meal in a Florentine restaurant that has been cooked by an Australian. In the enormous kitchen, two young girls assist me, while a series of dishwashers come and go. We wear pale-blue uniforms like nurses, and in quieter moments invent potent cocktails and bake batches of biscotti. By 11.30 p.m. the kitchen is packed up, gleaming, and I am dining either with my beloved or at the apartment wondering what time he will come home.

Our flat is just two rooms, tiny and purpose-built for restaurateurs who never cook at home, who work, live and eat at restaurants. Provision for the stove-top coffee maker and Gianfranco's collection of fancy liqueurs constitute the kitchen space. The other room is occupied exclusively by the double bed, above which presides a large television set, as if all a bedroom's purposes consist of sleeping, having sex and watching television – which, apart from the long nights I lie waiting for him to come home, is essentially all the entire flat is for.

My sister, who came here to be with me, often feels further away than if she were back in Australia. I know she is working as a sales assistant at a gold shop in Piazza Santa Croce and that she has put on twelve kilograms, but my self-absorption has blinded me to anything beyond that. Occasionally she comes in the car with us on day trips to the ocean; she sits in the back popping M&Ms into her mouth while Gianfranco teases her about her weight.

Subservience sits uneasily on me and I start to resent the fact that, after long, gruelling days running the restaurant, Gianfranco chooses the companionship of other men with

Penne with ricotta and spinach

For the sauce, blanch 300 g spinach, then squeeze dry. In a food processor, whizz the spinach together with 240 g ricotta and 1 tablespoon freshly grated Parmesan. Season with salt, pepper and nutmeg, and set aside. While pasta is cooking, dollop about a tablespoon per serving of the spinach/ricotta mix into a frying pan and add cream to extend it. Blend well to combine, check seasoning and gradually bring to the boil. Drain pasta, add to sauce, toss quickly to coat, then serve.

a pack of cards and whisky, while I am relegated to trophy status. When in a positive frame of mind, I manage to be philosophical about the hours I am left alone, in Florence or in his village, while he hooks up with old friends, attends to a business matter, or simply disappears. I am aware that I made the choice of both man and lifestyle, and of the privileges offered.

Yet, increasingly I find myself wading through impotence and incomprehension, like those dreams where your legs are clinging to a soaked and heavy garment and are struggling through the mud. I am so seriously in love that I have thrown out my contraceptive pills and I have had my blonde hair permed into a frizz to match Gianfranco's new hairdo. I am ironing his T-shirts. I suffer the interminable conversations, which swirl around me, about people and places I do not know. I am docile and stoic. I lie in our double bed in Via Osteria del Guanto waiting to hear the sound of Gianfranco's *motorino* as it turns into our narrow street. But the night deepens and empties, and still Gianfranco does not come home. I torment myself with imaginings and suspicions; I rewind details of the day as I try to trace back to where I may have given offence or let him down. There must have been something I did or said to make him value me less, to pretend I was not there, to exclude me, to stare through me, not answering my questions… when every fibre I possess shivers with the force of my adoring. I feel I have become another person.

The winter before he met me, Gianfranco had learned to ski. A new girlfriend is not going to impede this recently

41

discovered passion, and he tells me that I, too, will learn to ski. We head to one of Florence's smarter sports stores to fit me out. Because I have never skied in my life – nor been remotely tempted to do so – I have no idea what is required, but with his usual authority Gianfranco selects stretchy pants, zipped polo necks, a padded jacket so lovely I could weep, soft leather gloves and a cosy woollen hat, ski boots and shiny handsome skis. I try on this fancy costume, and in the shop mirror see a woman I do not recognise. Gianfranco pays for it all and I never find out if he subtracts the vast cost from my monthly *stipendio*. (That salary always seems inordinately large to me – two million lire! – and therefore somehow unreal. And because Gianfranco pays for everything, money is something I seem not to really need.)

And so commence the Wednesday trips to Abetone. The winter ski resort for Florentines, this village sits high in the Apennine Mountains above Pistoia, a ninety-minute drive from Florence. Four valleys link up to create ski slopes and cross-country runs through forests of firs, larches and pines. Figures fly past on skis and it is so beautiful that even before setting foot on the snow I am convinced I will love it.

Of course, the reality is quite different. Gianfranco teaches me the rudiments before sailing gracefully away, swallowed up in the frigid landscape. That first day I never stop falling over. I am appalled at my clumsiness and lack of coordination – I, who studied ballet for ten years, shone in aerobics classes and can still do the splits! Collapsed ignominiously in the snow, I feel discouragement seep into me. The warm spicy wine at the *rifugio* where I later meet up with Gianfranco restores my humour somewhat, and by the time the following Wednesday has come around I am prepared to publicly humiliate myself all over again.

Having only one day a week in order to learn a difficult sport like skiing at the reasonably seasoned age of twenty-eight means that progress is slow, painfully slow. In fact, every Wednesday I spend most of the day falling over, lolling abjectly in the snow longing for the whole ghastly ordeal to be over. Gianfranco finds it, and me, vastly entertaining. We always start out together and he is patient until I begin to sulk, at which point separation seems the most sensible idea, and off he sails.

And then, on the very last day we visit – winter on its way out and the snow patchier and thinner – something seems to snap into place. I have chosen a cross-country path through the trees, worn out by the steep slopes down which I mostly roll, flailing. Sun dances and dazzles and I have a clear, smooth passage ahead of me. I set off cautiously, increasing in confidence and speed, threading efficiently through the trees, my hips obeying – and suddenly I am flying, all fluid rhythm and calm, clear grace. It is one of the most exhilarating experiences of my life.

Val più la pratica che la grammatica
Experience is more important than theory

My Italian slowly improves, and yet, impeded by limited vocabulary, I remain frustrated by the inability to express my character and voice my opinions. For that first year I am perceived as quiet and acquiescent. I often feel like screaming out that I am really a strong, bubbly, opinionated, articulate and independent woman, and that in Australia most women are not required to sit for hours on end doing nothing while their partners are out hunting or playing cards or drinking with friends.

Gianfranco's closest friend is a waiter from Vecchia Toscana, married to a Russian woman. We go to their apartment for lunches, and when the business of eating is out of the way, the television is switched on for an afternoon's viewing of soccer, Formula 1 car racing or the sacred *calcio* – association football. Dulled by post-lunch liqueurs I slump in the darkened living room while cars roar around circuits and the air thickens with cigarette smoke. Olga, whose air of submission is probably as misinterpreted as mine, does not engage me in a female chat; we all stare at the screen.

Walrus-moustachioed Raimondo has left Antica Toscana, and has come to work at our restaurant. He is my ally. And so it is Raimondo to whom I turn after slicing my finger open, not to the man with whom I share my life who is up to day three in his silent treatment towards me. Our freshly laundered white aprons require perforated holes in the fabric for threading the ties. Generally, these perforations are effected with a knife. My little paring knife, newly sharpened, slips smoothly through first the starched fabric, then my finger. Blood shoots out. I have barely felt any pain and yet within seconds there is a heavy throbbing sensation, which I try to stem with a makeshift bandage. I find

Raimondo, who takes charge immediately, organising our absence from the restaurant for the following hour while he drives me to the nearest hospital.

It is just before lunchtime and Gianfranco is at a table with the other partners discussing the specials of the day. I stand in front of him with my throbbing finger and tell him what has happened and where I am about to be taken. I stand in front of him willing him to put his arms around me, to forgive me for whatever sexual transgression he believes I have committed, to remember he loves me. Instead, his eyes examine me like tiny black stones and I realise what has just happened has alienated him from me even further – that the inconvenience of my accident, indubitably an act of carelessness or stupidity, is merely adding to his contempt. He says not a word. Raimondo leads me gently away.

Inevitably, when I start to make sense of this world, the relationship begins to fall apart. This takes place painfully over many months, during which Gianfranco decides that I am being unfaithful to him. Unfaithful! I am so fiercely in love with him that the concept is almost laughable, except that his punishment is so severe. My sister has returned to Australia, and he is now the one I must rely on.

One afternoon he comes back to our apartment and does not greet me. He fails to respond to my concerned questions and looks right through me with hard, cold eyes. We go off to work together, and I am ignored for the evening. I am desperate with incomprehension and unhappiness. Back home, I wait and wait and wait, then eventually fall asleep, to awake at three o'clock or four o'clock in the morning to an empty bed. Days later, in his jeans pocket I find cards for out-of-town hotels that we have never been to together. The very fact that I am spying on him, not trusting him, searching for clues, appals me, and yet I cannot stop.

It is during one of these bouts of ostracism that I receive a rare phone call from Australia. At the sound of my mother's voice all I long to do is to pour out my sadness and my vulnerability, to hear her sensible voice and her unconditional love. But she is telling me about Tony, and how he had contacted her some weeks before, wanting my address in Florence. His plan was to travel to Europe via Bali – except he never got beyond Bali, because he drowned. He had gone out to one of the islands and somehow this former champion swimmer had drowned. Hearing about this good and gentle man whom I had discarded in my selfish urge for a larger, brighter life – hearing about it, furthermore, in the midst of yet another romantic crisis with the man who took his place – ushers in a bleakness as deep as it is lonely. I cannot even confide my grief in Gianfranco, because, at that time, I no more exist for him than Tony now does for me. I just fold it inside me.

Grande amore, grande dolore
Great love, great pain

Then one day he speaks to me; the wall of silence lifts. He accuses me of making love to the greengrocer in the mornings on my way to work. He is sick with jealousy, he tells me, and his excuse is that he is made that way. '*Io sono fatto così*' I hear a million times throughout that turbulent, glorious relationship, as if by saying those words he is giving himself permission to be as difficult, as cruel and as irrational as he likes.

Making up is so passionate that for a long time afterwards we are more in love than ever. My relief at being permitted to once more exist drowns out the utter absurdity of his accusations, and the danger of his paranoia. It turns into a pattern that is only broken after fifteen months, coinciding with both my beginning to dream in Italian, and, most significantly, finally turning back into myself. We break up just in time for my thirtieth birthday. Gianfranco drives me, the delicate invalid, out to Strada-in-Chianti outside Florence, to the sprawling country home belonging to our friends Vincenzo and Claudia to convalesce.

And so for several weeks all I do is sleep and read and help in the domestic kitchen. I go for long walks and eat a lot and dip Claudia's home-made almond biscotti into Vin Santo until late at night in the company of this infinitely kind couple who feel like my grandparents. They have known Gianfranco for many years and are not surprised it has turned out this way. Then one day I feel ready to re-enter the real world of work and relationships. I have no desire to follow my sister back to Australia. Florence has become home, and it is time to look for a job and a place to live.

Biscotti di prato
(Almond biscuits)

200 g almond kernels
500 g plain flour
Pinch salt
300 g caster sugar
1 teaspoon baking powder
2 eggs, plus 2 egg yolks
Grated rind 1 orange

*Toast almonds in moderate oven until crisp. Remove
and cool. In a large bowl, mix together flour, salt, sugar
and baking powder. Make a well in the centre and add
whisked eggs and yolks. Work together with hands to form
a smooth dough, then incorporate the almonds and orange
rind. Shape into 4 logs about 3 cm wide and set aside on
greased oven trays for about an hour, covered with a clean
tea towel. Glaze logs with extra beaten egg yolk, then bake
in 175°C (340°F, Gas mark 4) oven for about 30 minutes.
Remove and slice diagonally into 2 cm strips. Return to
oven and bake both sides 5 minutes each. Cool on trays.*

Nella guerra d'amore vince chi fugge
In the war of love he who escapes wins

I am sharing a flat in Via de' Barbadori with two students who study architecture at university. My bedroom is just large enough for a camp bed, a chest of drawers and a Pink Floyd poster. Each morning when I cross the Ponte Vecchio on my way to work at a tiny restaurant, the reflected shimmering of the ochre buildings in water stir me. The restaurant's name, I' Che C'è C'è, is colloquial Florentine, meaning 'What's there is there', suggesting pot luck as far as the food is concerned. And yet the new owner, Piero, has carefully composed a menu combining traditional meals with inspired modern flourishes. I am assistant chef to Maurizio, who used to work with – of course – Gianfranco. We are assisted in turn by Maurizio's mother, Emba.

Io sono aperta come una finestra in estate
I am as open as a window in summer

Emba is really everybody's mother. In her little girl's voice she calls us by her pet names. She is round and pinkly gleaming and huggable, except my arms do not reach all the way around her. She often describes someone as having a heart as big as a church, but no one I know deserves that accolade as much as she does. She is much more modest about herself. Another favourite expression of hers is, 'Io *sono aperta come una finestra in estate'* – 'I am as open as a window in summer'. Emba mainly washes up, but two of the pasta dishes on the menu use her special sauces, and our famous tiramisu, which she teaches me, is her own particular version.

We bump along together in the kitchen – Maurizio, with his heroin habit; la Veeky, finding another opportunity to make her cheesecakes; and Emba, who wears floral aprons from home and uses her wide, thick fingers to measure out ingredients. She aspirates the letter 'c' in true Florentine style, so that it comes out 'h', like the Florentine teenagers who ask for 'Hoha-Hola' when ordering a Coke.

Emba's hands scrape out the finely chopped herbs (thyme, tarragon, parsley) and onions from the food processor. Then she stirs them into her simmering tomato sauce before adding cream. This is the exquisite *salsa al'che c'è c'è*, which is tossed through pasta. The sauce is one of the reasons – along with our desserts – why this is a very busy restaurant. At the entrance of the kitchen she unzips her cloth purse and passes money to Maurizio. When he returns from his outing, he is white and sweaty and begins scrubbing, vigorously, the same square of bench-top for ten minutes as the orders pile up, his eyes pupil-less. Emba and I often manage the whole evening's cooking between us.

Piero is a tall dreamy teacher of Italian at the Leonardo da Vinci Institute who is trying his hand as restaurateur. His best invention is the *insalata al'che c'è c'è*, a mixture of finely shredded white cabbage, rocket leaves, toasted sesame seeds and grated salted ricotta. The latter comes from Sicily

Tiramisu all'arancia
(Orange tiramisu)

6 eggs
6 tablespoons caster sugar
500 g mascarpone
Grated rind 1 orange
Cold strong espresso coffee
Cocoa powder
Savoiardi biscuits

Separate the eggs, and whisk together the yolks with the sugar until well blended. Fold through mascarpone and orange rind until smooth. Separately, whisk egg whites until very stiff, then gently fold through mascarpone mixture until completely amalgamated. Dip savoiardi *into coffee and arrange one layer at the base of a bowl. Dollop in mascarpone cream and sprinkle with sifted cocoa powder. Continue these layers until the bowl is full, finishing with a generous layer of cocoa. Chill at least 4 hours, preferably overnight.*

and is hard and white, tangy and creamy all at once. Piero is passionate about cheese and chooses it with great care, as he does the interesting varieties of bread that we serve.

A parade of continental waitresses weaves in and out, most significantly fellow Australian Amanda (because she becomes a great friend) and Marie-Claire. Marie-Claire is chicly Parisian and is studying to be an art restorer – she cycles everywhere, her long legs pedalling underneath short, ruffled skirts.

Because it is restaurant life all over again, it remains a narrow one, with its one day off a week and its late nights, usually spent at other restaurants. Amanda and I often stay back at our restaurant when all the other staff have left, drinking and talking deep into the night. On my day off I am conscious that I am in Italy, where I could be day-tripping to places like Venice or Rome or Cinque Terre instead of wandering the supermarket aisles of UPIM trying to decide what shampoo to buy. There are parts of this beautiful city I know intimately, old tucked-away streets of herbalists and bookbinders and apothecaries and leather repairers. I know where all the good factory-seconds outlets are and the best bars for coffees and aperitifs. It has become a smaller, sweeter, safer world, in contrast to the turbulence that was Gianfranco.

Il primo amore non si scorda mai
You never forget your first love

Gianfranco begins a practice of dropping into I' Che C'è C'è each evening around five o'clock for coffee. He fills the doorway of the little kitchen and chatters to me as I set up for the evening. We have been apart for many months and I am feeling cured and strong, so why do I begin to anticipate the visits with excitement? It feels as if he is courting me again, and Marie-Claire and I start up a game of bets, in which if he comes she must pay me a thousand lire and if not I must pay her. I win lots of money. Late after work over Vin Ruspo and biscotti I have gradually confided the Gianfranco story to Marie-Claire, who listens with sympathy and, in turn, treats me to amusing accounts of her several ongoing affairs.

I am angry with myself for allowing this love to stir into life again. I remind myself how unhappy he made me, but all I am really conscious of are his eyes and his smile, the familiar fragrance of his aftershave, his crisp white shirts and easy laugh.

One evening he suggests dinner at Artimino, a gracious restaurant outside Florence where we went on one of our first dates. We will make a foursome with Marie-Claire and one of her current beaus. I am heady with happiness and hope. I dress carefully and, even when it transpires that it is just the three of us, because Marie-Claire's boyfriend cannot come, I am only briefly disappointed. We have the sort of special night out Gianfranco is so good at. He disappears into the restaurant kitchen, and when he reappears the menu is all worked out, full of fancy little dishes cooked exclusively for our table. Many fine wines are ordered and drunk, and upon my return from the toilet I am enchanted to see how well Gianfranco and Marie-Claire are getting on, and proud that I have introduced him to such a beautiful and interesting woman. The evening visits continue.

I know that Venice is considered almost lyrical in its loveliness, beloved of poets and writers throughout history. Thomas Mann said, 'To enter Venice by train is like entering a palace by the back door.' And a palace it is, although a palace whose richness and beauty is best appreciated outside of winter. For my first Christmas alone – no Gianfranco, friends otherwise occupied – I decide that I will distract myself by spending a week in Venice. I book myself into an inexpensive family-run pensione, and begin to feel excited.

It is the coldest winter Italy has experienced in decades. I am undeterred. I catch the train, arriving at the palace by the back door – and am nearly blown out of the compartment by the force of the icy wind. Because stoicism, a strong family trait, comes easily to me, I embrace the appalling weather as part of my next exciting adventure, the unconventional Christmas I will never forget. The fact that my pensione is shabby and austere – a single sagging bed in a narrow room with bidet and a solitary hook for my clothes – seems to render the adventure even greater. I check in and then spend a pleasurable time settling in, arranging toiletries on the shelf above the washbasin, alarm clock beside the bed, nightie under the musty pillow. Then it is time to launch into the outside world and explore this extraordinary city.

Years before I had come with a friend on a day in spring, a day trip of sunshine and magic. Over endless little bridges we loped, bewitched by the maze of mysterious little streets, the entrancing, majestic architecture, the thousands of pigeons in the Piazza San Marco – we even had the obligatory, outrageously priced coffee at Harry's Bar – but most of all by the fact that this was a city which floated on water, was built on water, would one day be overpowered and swallowed up by water. We knew it was a cliché, but could not help being infected by the joy on the faces of the newly wed couple posing for photographs in a gondola.

This time it is so utterly different I could be in another place altogether, except that it is all still there: the canals and the bridges, the architecture and the piazzas, the majesty and the mystery. The water is all choppy, angry waves whipped into peaks by the wind, which never drops. Few people are out, and those who dare are wrapped in eminently more sensible clothing than I – the sort of clothing you wear at a ski resort, perhaps. And, to be sure, there is snow – dirty yellow heaps of it piled in corners. All I want to do is get out of the wind so that I can think, compose myself, recover my good humour, plan where I will go for my evening meal. I erupt gratefully into a bar and ponder my possibilities. It is early afternoon and grey, grey, grey, and I have at least five hours before a lovely dinner somewhere can rescue me. I know there are the Doge's Palace and the Campanile and the Rialto Market within walking distance; there are literary walks I could set out on and Tintorettos everywhere to marvel at. All of these things on a mild calm day I would exuberantly do, and yet looking out the window of the bar at the bleak, unpopulated landscape the only way I can think to cheer myself up is to return to the pensione and slide into bed with a book.

In bed with a book is mostly how the first three days of my Christmas in Venice pass. The icy wind becomes a permanent part of each day I so optimistically rise and prepare for. It drives me out of the pensione and into a shop, bar, café or restaurant from whose warm interiors I never want to emerge. Spending so much money in these refuges means I spend increasing time in the narrow lumpy bed, reading gloomily. I cheer up briefly around six o'clock in the evening, when I sit perched and purposeful in a snug little trattoria, reading the menu over a carafe of house wine, scribbling down brooding thoughts and observations in my notebook, sliding the day back into perspective.

On the fourth day I can bear it no longer. I am miserable – the sun has not appeared once in all that time – and homesick for my funny little cupboard of a bedroom in Florence, for my sweet flatmates with whom I visualise sharing Pandoro and spumante in the Christmas spirit I so shockingly do not feel. Florence could not possibly be as vacant and joyless as Venice for a lonely woman alone. I do not even consider the waste of the week paid for as I board the train home.

It is the end of the year, and both Gianfranco's restaurant and I' Che C'è C'è have planned special banquets for New Year's Eve. We are fully booked. Most of the day I am in the kitchen with Maurizio and Emba preparing complicated antipasti, creamy smoked salmon sauces for pasta, cannelloni stuffed with nutmeggy ricotta and spinach, *cotechino* (pork sausage) with lentils and roasted game, anchovy sauce to eat with steak. Emba is making her famous orange biscotti: dough pungent with orange rind, rolled into coils, then deep-fried to a sticky gold crispness. I have an irresistible urge to see Gianfranco halfway through the day to find out how his preparations are going. I suspect he is lunching, as he mostly does, at Vecchia Toscana, and so I set off, grateful to be away from the steamy, hectic kitchen for half an hour or so. As I approach the restaurant, I see Marie-Claire's bicycle leaning against the wall by the entrance. When I find Gianfranco, in one of the dining rooms, she is sitting next to him eating lunch, and one of her legs coils around his, like a snake.

Piero decides to replace his head chef the evening Maurizio pushes through the beaded curtains separating the kitchen from the dining room and threads his way between crowded tables to the front door, where he exits for the Piazza Signora and a fix. It is *mezzo servizio*, the middle of service: the restaurant is full and I am alone in the kitchen except for David, the Israeli dishwasher, and a pile of orders to be filled, which we somehow bluff our way through. The dining customers have no idea that the meals sent out have been cobbled together by an assistant chef and the 'dish-pig' because the head chef has left the premises.

A series of chefs come to I' Che C'è C'è, clutching their toolboxes filled with knives. They spend a day each in our small kitchen, showing off their technical skills, while Emba and I hover anxiously, feeling homespun and shabby and disliking them all. Only one of them teaches me something useful, which is to take a whisk to those tinned tomatoes still stubbornly retaining their shape after half an hour

Acciugata
(Anchovy sauce)

Clean fresh anchovies and remove the central bone.
Heat olive oil in a frypan over moderately high heat
and add the anchovies. With a fork, squash them
until they break up and become a thick sauce. Serve
a dollop onto grilled steak or alongside fish.

simmering toward a sauce. For all their trade certificates, none of them seems capable of the *casalinga* – homely – touch for which we are known and loved... until Fabrizio presents himself.

Fabrizio is a short, neat man whose late middle age has been tidied away beneath tinted glasses and a hairpiece. He dresses impeccably in starched whites and his movements are crisp and economical. Emba and I adore him immediately, and so he is hired. We quickly learn that he is married but has a lover in the outer Florentine suburb of Sesto Fiorentino. The fact that he tipples away at cooking wine is unimportant. When he is a little drunk, he inserts one index finger into his right cheek, pops it out with a small explosion and announces, *'Sciampagna per tutti'* – Champagne all round. Another one of his sayings, after he has created a dish of which he is especially proud, is *'Nemmeno in Giappone lo fanno cosi!'* – not even in Japan do they make it like this! And after a while the rest of us adopt *'Stentalett'*, his invented, meaningless term of affection. Fabrizio cooks calmly, with an air of irony and detachment. Some afternoons he steps down from the kitchen to greet a thick-set woman whose large black handbag clutched to her chest seems to want to hide her. They are brief and formal together, and when Fabrizio returns to the kitchen, he murmurs, *'Sesto Fiorentino,'* and winks.

Into the Via de' Barbadori apartment move the Israeli dishwasher and his sewing machine. We are amiably overcrowded and yet somehow retain our little territories, our separate lives. One student eats formally prepared meals on his own, snapping off neat segments of the hollow bread rolls he loves before retiring to his bedroom to discuss projects with fellow students around his architect's table. The other is soft and blond and lazy, and leaves the apartment around ten o'clock most evenings to go *in giro* – cruise around – with his more fashionable friends, usually ending up at discotheques.

David the Israeli dishwasher and I discover a great point of intimacy: ice cream. Talking about ice cream reveals surprising areas of David's soul, a soul I otherwise think of as bruised and blackened as old fruit in this taciturn and hardened ex-soldier. A stocky man balding young, he walks bent forward, looking hunted and furtive. His clothes – tight jeans, loose polo necks, bulky jackets with padded shoulders and obscure labels stitched to the sleeves – are all black. Pointed black shoes tap out at right angles as he walks over the bridge to Gailli *gelateria* and takes his place alongside the line of ice cream buyers in front of the window. His favourites are chocolate mousse, chocolate *stracciatella* and a particularly alcoholic flavour based on rum. Three scoops are smeared into a paper cup and stabbed with a tiny plastic spoon, coins transferred, and David is tapping back over the bridge. The ice cream is finished before he has arrived back at the apartment, a few minutes' walk away. This is not only the best ice cream in Florence, it is the best ice cream in the world.

One mid-afternoon, the sun is slanting through the slats of Venetian blinds and running stripes down David's black T-shirt. He is sitting at the vintage sewing machine he bought when he decided that it was fashion rather than stage sets he wished to design, head bent over the chattering needle and oblivious to my entrance, the fabric bunched up and spilling off the polished old wood of the machine.

When David was a soldier in the Israeli army, he once stormed into a hotel and shot a man dead. Maybe there were others he killed – maybe after he has seen my look of horror, he decides not to tell me about the others. We do not know each other very well. I have never met someone who has killed another person: it is the first thing I know about David and seems to explain his tough, squat body and premature balding, his black attire, the endless cigarettes he hand-rolls, an absence of smiling and rare laughter behind closed teeth; hands plunged in pockets while taking coffee at a bar standing silent amongst strangers. He has hard, pale eyes and hollow cheeks, a stony, chiselled beauty but an unapproachability. I see the young, raw drama student painting sets and dreaming of theatre and flamboyant costumes tossed suddenly into war. One day he kills a man with a rifle blast and ever after carries around that one, sharp shot that hardens the line of his jaw.

There we both are one August evening, lined up together at the Gailli window. Through the glass are the stainless-steel tubs containing ice cream whipped to glossy peaks, studded with nuts, chocolate, angelica, cherries, toffee, caramel, laced with liqueurs, luridly pink and green and gold and purple, white like snow, rippled with berries. I am attempting to control my greed as I select flavours. David, who has no inhibitions where ice cream is concerned, is simply selecting flavours.

Walking back home over the bridge to the apartment (which up until then we have shared politely as strangers) we spoon ice cream into our mouths and become friends. Finding someone who shares your passion is almost like falling in love. Enthusiasm bounces back and forth between us, radiating the air – our smiles are rich with understanding. The details to discuss are myriad: I can suddenly confide my thoughts on texture and temperature, our ice cream conversations intense as we describe the eating sensation as we might describe love-making.

But ice creams are not enough. In the end David always slides back into his impenetrability, his head bent over the sewing machine, his Middle Eastern cassettes swirling mystically, his secret soldier's self tidied away. And yet I know that softness is there – I have listened to him describe the colour of taste, and the taste of colour, and known exactly what he meant.

It is about one and a half hours by train from Florence to Riccione. I am taking a brief vacation with a German girl I barely know, beautiful Simone, who is staying in our apartment on a camp bed in the cramped living room. We are booked into the Hotel Souvenir, a modestly priced establishment a short walk from the beach.

It is August, the middle of summer. Riccione is one of the most popular seaside resorts on the Riviera Romagnola, the stretch of coast running from the Po River Delta to Cattolica. I read somewhere that it is known as *'la perla verde dell'Adriatico'* – the green pearl of the Adriatic – but there is nothing pearly-green about the flat, lank ocean. So accustomed am I to the majesty and the beauty of Australian beaches – transparent water and infinite expanses of fine white sand, towering waves and bush-backed dunes – that the vision before me of neat, endless rows of deckchairs, umbrellas, chaises longues and towels seems to be a colourful cartoon. Furthermore, we are required to rent our small allotment of sand. We choose the cheapest option, a tidy space on which to extend our beach towels. Simone immediately unhooks the bra of her bikini and offers her oiled Teutonic limbs to the sun, and I am aware of the bronzed gods bouncing a soccer ball nearby glancing over towards our spot at regular intervals.

I am delighted anyway, regardless of my inability to take this concept of beach seriously. Hundreds of bodies stand waist-deep in the muggy, murky water engaged in conversation and laughter, surrounded by children who flop and thrash inside flotation devices. All along the tree-lined seafront boulevard stand hotels, side by side, their gardens cooled by awnings and parasols with chairs facing the sea.

Simone is vain and moody, I realise quickly, and yet her company is agreeable, even if the desultory conversations we conduct in our flawed Italian never touch on topics deeper than clothes and men. After hours of comatose sunbaking, we sit out the front of our hotel spooning cherry and turquoise-coloured *gelato* into our mouths from long shapely glasses, and in the evenings over a carafe of Trebbiano we eat seafood, scooping up the spicy sauces with thin ovals of bread called *piadina*. We catch the bus to Rimini, fifteen minutes away, and prowl around the historic centre of the old town, which dates back to the first century before Christ. My hair is bleached nearly white, and we flaunt our lubricated tans beneath skimpy beach dresses, but every evening when we set out for dinner I notice how effortlessly Simone slides on cream linens and fluttery silks, transforming into the chic and sophisticated European woman I will never manage to be.

The circle of cross-cultural visitors widens: Danish, American, German and Irish friends; Amanda and her sculptor husband, Rex; occasionally Raimondo, who has become my anti-Marie-Claire crusader – or, more accurately, the great Vicky-and-Gianfranco supporter, despite my protestations of never again, never again. Raimondo, who loved us as a couple, loves to reminisce about the summer night the three of us – he, Gianfranco and I – headed off from the restaurant as drunk as lords and drove to Viarreggio singing 'Maremmo maremma mare' the entire way, fell asleep on the beach upon arrival, and awakened mid-morning, as fiercely sunburnt as we were hung over.

An Australian friend visits and we play endless rounds of Travel Scrabble, dreading the moment we hear the metallic clank of the ancient lift as it reaches our top floor and the grilled door grinds open, releasing an interruption in the form of visitors.

One Sunday night the lift cage bears unexpected visitors. I know Antonella vaguely – she is the sister of a friend – but I had only heard about her Sicilian boyfriend. Cesare towers over everyone. His thick hair, as black as his eyes, cascades past his shoulders. They interrupt each other to tell me about the restaurant they have bought at Portoferraio, on the Isle of Elba; it is to be called Robespierre and will focus on seafood. They are currently interviewing, and am I interested in coming over for the summer as assistant chef?

There is an apartment organised for us all to share, right in the heart of Portoferraio, a five-minute walk from the restaurant.

I have been to Elba once, for several days of sunshiny holiday in the early stages of Gianfranco. I remember the ferry across from the mainland, a little island you can drive around in three hours, yachts bobbing lazily in the port, an ocean transparently blue. I consider the cosy eventlessness of my life. I am conscious, mostly, of bovine contentment. Wherever I end up, in whatever city or country, I am always soaking clothes in a bucket in the bathroom, spraying on tester perfumes in department stores, planning a new diet and keeping gloomy diaries. Each morning I buy *La Nazione* from the same news-stand and gulp down a tepid cappuccino from the corner bar; lately at night, standing in front of the refrigerator as the rest of the apartment sleeps, I have found myself eating mascarpone straight out of its tub as if to feed some bottomless pocket of emptiness. Because I never seem free of that little pocket, I say yes.

Per non litigare occorre rimanere celibi
In order not to have arguments
you should remain single

The view out of my bedroom window is of the faded, peeling yellow buildings with wooden green shutters and the squat boxy entrance to the *panificio* where we buy bread rolls and loaves for the restaurant. There is a plaque to Victor Hugo on the wall of the town hall, and a pizzeria called Garibaldino.

Robespierre has three-cornered hats for lampshades and a wooden guillotine at the entrance, built by Cesare. It has clothed tables inside and out. For the opening Gianfranco catches the ferry over and spends the day creating culinary art. A whole baked fish with potato scales reposes on a platter; overlapping curls of crimson prosciutto spiral into a tower crowned by a basket of parsley sculpted out of an orange; prawns, shrimps and scampi tumble amongst radish rosettes. We await the arrival of our new chef, Annunzio.

Annunzio, a widower, comes from Cecina on the mainland, where he lives with his only daughter. He looks like a villain from an old-fashioned melodrama, with his slicked-back hair and his bloodshot eyes and his huge nicotine-stained teeth; spittle glistens and sprays when he speaks. Elastic braces stretch around his great belly and he wears long-sleeved undergarments and sad, iron-creased jeans with open-toed sandals and socks. Struck by his ugliness and his oddness, I am briefly daunted by the prospect of sharing a flat with him. Annunzio is nearly ready for retirement, but he has decided that Robespierre shall be his swan song. We are a strange quartet: Antonella and Cesare prickly with sexual tension and drug-induced mood swings, la Veeky on a yoghurt diet grimly determined to put Gianfranco behind her, and gentle, humming, yarn-spinning, eccentric Annunzio.

We settle in. Quickly I acquire a boyfriend, part-owner of the Garibaldino pizzeria. He takes me to open-air discotheques around the island, then back to a parked caravan, where he efficiently makes love to me. I am also flattered by the attentions of his *pizzaiolo*, who is ten years younger than me and who, despite his Dutch girlfriend, comes to park himself on his Vespa outside the back door of Robespierre to flirt with me. He is dazzlingly beautiful. After a while, when the four of us – the pizza boys and their foreign girlfriends – take to frequenting a wine bar after work, I find myself not minding the younger one's hand on my thigh beneath the table; my animated conversation with his girlfriend does not falter. I have gone a little crazy – a combination of a languidly hot summer, the sense that nothing taking place on the island is real, and a pathetic need to be loved.

I buy a second-hand pushbike, and each afternoon at the end of service pedal along the streets that lead to my favourite beach. I step out of my sticky, sweaty, oily work clothes and plunge into the crisp ocean, where, after swimming vigorously for some time, I float on my back, weightless, deaf, eternal. When I return to my neatly folded pile of clothes, I stretch out on the towel and promptly fall asleep, for precisely one hour. Then it is time to bicycle back to the apartment, to shower and dress and prepare for the evening's work.

Mangia che ti passa
Eat and you will feel better

Annunzio soaks his underwear in Omino Bianco bleach; returning to our apartment, I see the line of large, blindingly white, square underpants and billowing singlets that marks his bedroom window. Each evening before work, he and I pause briefly for a *spumantino* at the same bar.

At night, after Annunzio and I have scrubbed the kitchen down, we set up a small table and two chairs out the back of the kitchen and have our dinners. I only ever eat two things, which I alternate: char-grilled swordfish with Annunzio's lemon-olive oil emulsion drizzled over the top, or bulgy buffalo mozzarella sliced with ovals of sweet San Marzano tomatoes and spicy basil. This, too, is Annunzio's favourite meal, the tomatoes at their peak of ripeness, their glossy egg shapes sliced vertically and arranged over the cheese.

All Annunzio's movements are ponderous. He rotates his thick fingers slowly over the plate, salt and pepper scattering. The basil leaves, the new green olive oil and, then, the slow messy business of eating – teeth clicking, oil spraying, bread sopping up the juices and gumming his conversation. We both eat too much bread and drink too much wine, and then wander, two unlikely friends, down to Bar Roma at the water's edge to sit watching the boats. Annunzio tells me stories from his life over his baby whisky; I spoon pistachio-green *gelato* into my mouth from a silver dish and feel safe and very young.

Annunzio's stories all follow the same pattern: past restaurants he has owned or managed, which failed, leaving him jobless, defeated, disillusioned and desperately poor. People he had trusted who had turned their backs; countries he had lived in, whose languages he had learned, which had finally disenchanted him. The woman he should have married and whom he still loves, instead of the sick woman who is his wife. His huge yellow teeth seem to bite something – perhaps the air – as he speaks. The clicking boats with lives of their own, their rhythmic nodding, canvas clapping, are like some massive beast slumbering restlessly. That he can make me feel like this – sweet, somehow, and pure, and uncorrupted – is one of the best reasons for loving him.

On my day off, I begin with a sticky, jam-filled croissant and cappuccino at the bar near the newsstand. Then I head off on the bicycle to the beach. I feel blonde, brown, free and promiscuous, and only saved from self-loathing by the tacit forgiveness Annunzio offers me each night when he so cosily buys me ice cream.

Annunzio's blunt fingers press mixture into splayed sardines. *L'impasto* consists of bread soaked in milk, finely chopped parsley and garlic, ground mortadella, grated Parmesan, sultanas and pine nuts. He shows me how to pinch up the sides of the sardines and place them in neat rows in a baking tray, slipping a bay leaf in between each. Then he splashes white wine over the top and bakes them.

A similar mixture fills mussel shells. The mussels are steamed quickly (olive oil, garlic and parsley, a dash of wine) until they open. Half the double shell is discarded and the mussel in the remaining one packed snugly with milk-soaked breadcrumbs, garlic and parsley and grated Parmesan. These are baked until golden brown. Another batch of mussels simmers in a basic tomato sauce into which a little dried chilli is crumbled. These dishes form the basis of the antipasto table that stands at the back of the Robespierre. My favourite is the platter of fresh raw anchovies, which start out pink and plump and end up gleaming a bright white under Annunzio's emulsion of lemon juice and olive

Sarde al beccafico
(Baked stuffed sardines)

2 slices day-old rustic bread
Milk
2 tablespoons sultanas
2 tablespoons pine nuts
80–100 g mortadella, as finely chopped as possible
2 tablespoons Grana or Parmesan, freshly grated
Grated rind 1 lemon
2 fat cloves of garlic, finely chopped
2/3 bunch parsley, finely chopped
Salt and pepper
750 g fresh sardines, filleted and butterflied
Bay leaves
White wine
Olive oil

Preheat oven to 200°C (400°F, Gas mark 6). Soak bread in
milk briefly, then squeeze dry. Place in a bowl together with
sultanas, pine nuts, mortadella, cheese, lemon rind, garlic
and parsley, season with salt and pepper and combine well.
Place about a teaspoon of mixture in the middle of each
sardine and arrange on baking tray with a bay leaf either
side. Sprinkle wine over the top and drizzle with olive oil.
Bake for 10 to 15 minutes. Serve as part of an antipasto.

oil, and a scattering of chopped parsley. In a giant vat, Annunzio simmers a huge octopus in red wine for hours. The particular aroma of caramel remains in my nostrils long afterwards. Then Annunzio slips off the skin, chops the fat tentacles into chunks and tosses together a salad with fresh herbs and a touch of chilli.

Apart from assisting Annunzio with the antipasti, my job is, as usual, the *primi* – the pasta dishes – and the desserts. I love preparing pasta with the *scoglio* sauce, which, unlike most others, is made to order. Before me I have containers of well-scrubbed mussels, clams, pipis, date mussels and Venus clams soaking in water. There is a separate container of finely chopped garlic and parsley, which I dollop into a pan of sizzling olive oil. When the aromas rise, I throw in handfuls of shellfish and toss them around before splashing in white wine. Meanwhile the pasta is cooking; once it is al dente, it is drained quickly, added to the pan of clinking shellfish, mixed briefly, then toppled out onto plates.

Strawberry risotto is fashionable this year, and at the height of summer it remains fixed on our specials board. The strawberries are simply puréed, seasoned with salt and pepper, then stirred through towards the finish of a plain risotto, a little grated cheese and butter added at the very end. A silly sort of dish, but very popular, particularly when served alongside shiny-black squid-ink risottos, which we often do. On my boyfriend's birthday, he comes for lunch and I send out his strawberry risotto in the shape of a heart.

Annunzio is an oasis of calm and wisdom. Around him Cesare, Antonella and I flap hectically from one mistaken experiment to another, while the summer blazes on. Cesare and Antonella have spectacular rows in the middle of the restaurant while customers dine. Cesare's long legs in loose trousers stride off, contemptuously, leaving Antonella crumpled.

The pizzeria owner and I drift apart after the evening we lie side by side in his sordid caravan discussing the beauty of certain people we know. I am bold – rash enough – to ask if he thinks I am beautiful, to which, without hesitation, he replies, 'No, you're not beautiful, but you are a character.' I am wounded, of course, especially because it has always seemed to me that people for whom you feel affection attain a kind of beauty; being a character strikes me as a very poor consolation prize. The *pizzaiolo* and I find ourselves together one late afternoon, sitting on a cliff looking out at the ocean, the luxury of being alone at last, with suddenly nothing to talk about and desire which has shrivelled.

I flip in and out of one-night stands, and the night Gianfranco comes over to visit we both drink a lot, then go down to the midnight beach together. Our clothes come off quickly and we make love in wet sand. I feel a brief, gloating victory over the absent Marie-Claire, but mostly a sense of familiar disappointment with myself. Down at Bar Roma over drinks and ice cream, I describe my life to Annunzio in veiled vague terms I will him to see through, and he always does, which afterwards comes to me as a sort of blessing. '*È una vacanza,*' he often reassures me – it is a holiday – excusing my promiscuity on the grounds that it is not real life.

BOOK ONE

A lanky boy from Brescia arrives to do our washing-up. As I cycle away to the beach at three o'clock, I leave him sitting in my chair at the little table opposite Annunzio. When another Australian friend comes over to the island to visit, she and the new dishwasher sit on the seawall long after the rest of us have left the pizzeria. They sit there all night and talk – or at least that is my friend's version. At any rate, they fall in love. Yet another friend flies back for a visit, and over Travel Scrabble in her pensione room she tells me how her new affair is progressing. Bells toll across the piazza on the half-hour and I am conscious of being frozen in one of my pointless limbo periods with no idea what to do next, while all around me others are radiant with self-definition or love. Sometimes I visit a trattoria for solitary dinners, leaving the dishwasher and Annunzio to explore the meaning of the universe while the owner flirts with me and I respond politely.

Toward the end of the season Gianfranco pays another visit. He is businesslike: the three partners of his restaurant would like me to join the partnership, returning to my old stomping ground and running the kitchen there. Our mutual friend Signore Lorenzo has offered to put up the money for my part. Gianfranco and Marie-Claire plan to leave on a holiday to Chile in October and it would suit him enormously if I could be back in Florence by then. I have never been able to deny him anything, and I find nothing has changed. Besides, it is time to move on, away from the illusory nature of island life and its encircling waters that shimmer like a mirage.

L'amore domina senza regole
Love rules without rules

The Florentine restaurant still serves endless busloads of tourists ('group food' is my somewhat disparaging term for the meals we send out to them), and still has its eclectic international menu. An interesting addition is the baked *provola* served in various ways. Ramekins, lined with thick slices of this soft smoky cheese, are topped with anchovies, pancetta, raw eggs or porcini mushroom sauce and then slid into the oven until melted and bubbling.

But the hamburgers remain as popular as ever. I am reminded of a car trip to the coast, those early days with Gianfranco and three other men I did not know. We were off to see an exciting new hamburger joint, and as we drove one of the men was describing the wall panel behind the counter, which consisted of colour photographs of the range of hamburgers available. When we finally arrived I was the only one not leaping about with enthusiasm; privately I was feeling a sense of disenchantment that a country whose culinary traditions I venerated so highly could so easily be seduced by the trashy culture of the disposable.

I am surprised at how effortlessly I slip back in, despite mostly new staff. Raimondo is still there entertaining customers with his Frankie Banana persona, muttering darkly about the witch Marie-Claire to me, wheeling me away to Yellow pizzeria after work for sausage calzoni and too many bottles of white Corvo. And then there is Ignazio.

BOOK ONE

I am lying in my old bed in Gianfranco's flat, which he has asked me to mind for him the week he and Marie-Claire are away. I am in my old bed, in my old flat, but I am too thick with cold to feel bitter or wistful. On my 'Back to Florence' diet, which consists of eating diet biscuits for breakfast, lunch and dinner for as long as I can stand it, I have also doped myself up with cough and cold tablets. On the television set is a programme of video clips, and as I watch I suddenly see a beautiful, familiar face on the screen. The group is Duran Duran and the face belonging to the lead singer bears an uncanny resemblance to the young waiter Ignazio.

In this state of buzzy hyperreality I find myself floating into a fantasy in which I am seducing this waiter to whom I have barely spoken. The following evening at work, after my ten o'clock beer (I slip so easily back into routines), I hear myself saying to Ignazio, who has come up to the kitchen window bearing empty plates, how much I would love to seduce him. He smiles his exquisite cherubic smile and departs, leaving me both terrified and excited by my impulse. I clear up the kitchen in a sort of trance, barely conscious of my actions, pondering consequences of crazy notions. When he returns a little later, I say, as calmly as I can manage, 'So, what do you think?' and he tells me he had not heard what I had said. Now I am in a position of great embarrassment; the only recourse is to plough on, and so I repeat my original sentence, and am gratified by a blush that suffuses his entire face and down his neck. 'All right,' is what he says, as if I had suggested we go for a *gelato*! He is seventeen years old to my thirty-one.

Two years living in Italy have, in a sense, merely perpetuated the pattern of my entire life, a reactive progression from one set of circumstances or opportunities to the next. No five-year plans, no long-term projects, no real ambitions unless you counted the cloudy, inchoate one of writing – for which a full, colourful and even accidental life has always seemed imperative. Ours was not an ambitious family. Ambition was never a particular value, unlike season tickets to the opera and ballet and book vouchers when we excelled at school. Nor were we a family to whom property and things mattered, doubtless explaining the ease with which all my adult life I had moved from one rental accommodation to another, from city to city, my one asset a superior stereo system. I had first come to this country to study the language, and then I fell in love. When that ended I found myself somehow engaged with the community and people around me; jobs were offered and the minutiae of ordinary, diurnal life distracted me from the larger questions. Now love had struck again.

A tavola non si invecchia
At the table, one does not age

Ignazio and I are a secret for a long time. What begins as a game, a joke, a fantasy, transforms into a real affair. He is my Botticelli angel – he is the most beautiful person I have ever known. Back in Via de' Barbadori he squashes in beside me in my box-like bedroom; the following morning I wrap my arms around his waist as we putter off to work on his silver-blue Vespa. I take photographs of him naked, his dark-brown eyes like the liquid centres of the chocolates he is eating. It seems to me that I have captured on film the essence of sensuality.

We are discreet: I especially dread Gianfranco finding out, fearful of being laughed at in general. I am too old, he is too young – facts which, when we are together exploring minds and bodies, are of no interest or issue. Besides, this is no great passion like the Gianfranco affair. I am cosy, serene and secure with Ignazio, re-establishing vast tracts of self-confidence in my unfamiliar role as teacher.

Raimondo is the first to find out, dropping around unexpectedly in the middle of the afternoon at the precise moment that Ignazio, shrouded in my bathrobe, is leaving the bedroom. He is shocked, of course, but adjusts with some amusement to the situation once the three of us are sitting at I' Che C'è C'è eating *fettuccine alla boscaiola* over lots of celebratory wine. After a while, I cease to care about the opinions of others.

One day, urbane Lorenzo, owner of Antica Toscana and devoted family man, pokes his head through the kitchen window and calls me over. He tells me that he has a proposition to put to me, but it is private. Would we be able to meet to discuss it the following evening? I am intrigued, flattered, a little discomfited, but we agree to meet outside I' Che C'è C'è at nine o'clock. I have always adored Lorenzo, his avuncular nature and his kind eyes behind thick glasses and his paternal fondness for Gianfranco. I was enchanted when he returned from a trip to Peru, bringing me back an

Fettuccine alla boscaiola
(Fettuccine of the forest)

Olive oil
1 medium onion, finely chopped
2–3 cloves garlic, finely chopped
2 cups finely sliced button mushrooms
White wine
400 g peeled and chopped tomatoes
1/2 cup water
Salt and pepper
1/2–1 cup cream
Parsley to garnish

Heat olive oil in pan and add onion and garlic, cooking
over moderate heat until softened (about 8 to 10 minutes).
Add mushrooms and cook on high heat, stirring frequently.
When they have given up most of their liquid, slosh in about
1/3 cup wine and allow to evaporate. Throw in tomatoes
and extra water, season and bring to the boil, then lower
heat to simmer for about 40 minutes, topping up with water
if reducing too much. Check seasoning. Allow about 2/3
cup sauce per serving and add cream according to taste,
blending in well. Toss through cooked, drained pasta on high
heat, then serve garnished with finely chopped parsley.

exquisite alpaca jumper. What can he possibly be proposing to me, which is to be kept from Gianfranco and presumably the other partners of the restaurant? I am eternally grateful to him for having financially enabled me to join the partnership, even if I have no understanding of why they want me as a partner or of the formalities (the sitting through important meetings in the solemn offices of solicitors and accountants pretending to comprehend, placing my signature confidently at the bottom of indecipherable documents, with absolute faith that Gianfranco would always look after me). My final guess is that Lorenzo wishes to set up another restaurant, would like me to work there but wants to hear my thoughts before telling the others. Ignazio and I discuss this at great length, and the following evening we dine quite early at I' Che C'è C'è before he heads back to the flat to await my return.

At nine o'clock, I step outside the restaurant and in a matter of minutes Lorenzo's sleek car pulls up. We drive for a long time until we reach the outskirts of Florence, where Lorenzo parks outside a nondescript restaurant. I am a little bewildered by the hushed formality of the interior as we are led to a table. A trolley appears with a smoked salmon on it. One elderly waiter thinly slices it as another one dribbles spumante into two flutes. I am too embarrassed to tell Lorenzo that I have already dined, that I have no room to eat anything more. I eat and drink politely and slowly, and we talk about generalities. It is only towards the end of an hour that I summon the courage to ask Lorenzo what it is he wishes to propose to me. His eyes magnify behind his spectacles; he looks almost sad. He would like to take me away sometime soon, to Sardinia perhaps or down to Capri, just a weekend he can arrange off for me. Then he would like to find me a nice little apartment somewhere in central Florence where I can be my own person and not have to share with university students.

I am listening to this in a state of horror, which politeness prevents me from betraying. How can I have misunderstood a situation quite so spectacularly? Have I missed little signs that may have been leading to this? Suddenly his financial backing and the glorious alpaca jumper are no longer the well-meaning gestures of a kindly uncle figure at all. I murmur platitudes of gratitude, then explain, carefully, that I am involved with someone and therefore not in the position to accept his kind offers. The evening ends abruptly. We leave shortly afterwards, driving the long way back in shrieking silence, and when Lorenzo drops me by the Ponte Vecchio there is none of the urbane door-opening which prefixed our evening. I feel literally dropped off, and as his car spins off into the night I run as fast as I can over the bridge and up Via de' Barbadori and into the lift and through the door of the apartment. In my bedroom, Ignazio lies asleep in the single bed. I sit down beside him and look at him. I seem to be looking at all the innocence, sweetness and uncorruptedness in the world, and when I touch the softness of his arm his long, spiky eyelashes separate and his beautiful brown eyes are looking at me with adoration. I have never loved him more.

Ignazio and I move into an apartment in Via Ghibellina, behind the Duomo and a few doors up from the Michelangelo

Institute. That summer I climb up through the ceiling and onto the roof, where I spread a towel and sunbake in a landscape of shimmering spires and terracotta. Ignazio and I lie in bed eating Vivoli *gelato* out of big tubs; we play Scrabble in Italian and I teach him English. When the restaurant closes for renovations, we fly to Egypt for a holiday, sailing on feluccas, staying at the hotel in Aswan, where *Death on the Nile* was filmed, visiting tombs in the Valley of the Dead, buying perfumed oils in tiny stoppered bottles.

We began in Cairo with a slap-up night at the Nile Hilton. Before setting off to explore the city the following morning, flushed with the extravagance that characterises the beginnings of vacations, we order the Sultan's Breakfast – a banquet wheeled in on a trolley.

Cairo is a cacophony of cars, donkeys and goats competing for space on illogical road systems. We visit the Museum of National Antiquities and later lurch off on camels through smoky sunshine on the city's outskirts towards the Pyramids of Giza. The guide tells us that Napoleon calculated there would be enough stones in the three main pyramids alone to build a three-metre-high wall around the whole of France. I nearly faint on the narrow circular staircase winding up inside the Great Pyramid of Cheops, pressed sweatily between large German bottoms and vigorous American thighs. We gaze at the sprawling splendour of the Sphinx and purchase little scrolls of printed papyrus from the Papyrus Institute.

From Cairo we catch the train and follow the Nile down to Luxor, a village-city whose very name evokes dusty musky sensuousness. We visit the bewilderingly vast architecture of the Karnak temple complex and roam through the bleak and arid landscape of the Valley of the Kings; at night we eat carp and rice washed down by pink wine that tastes like turpentine. Aswan is our end of the Nile; we had hoped to travel as far down as the High Dam at Abu Simbel, but the minute we glimpse the Old Cataract Hotel we decide we are going to stay there for ever. We sit on the cool verandahs of this enormous orangey-pink Moorish-style building sipping gin and tonics, staring at giant palms in gracious grounds and the Nile before us with its gently bobbing feluccas.

Of course, we know we cannot stay for ever at the Old Cataract – we must return to Rome and our ordinary lives, and we still have a week in which to explore the Red Sea. And so we catch the bus through a monotony of desert, Ignazio ashen-faced from the stomach cramps he has mysteriously incurred overnight. From there it is – and we should have read the signs – downhill all the way.

It is by the Red Sea that I throw away our return air tickets to Rome. More accurately, it is in the foyer of the Sheraton Hotel just outside the Egyptian deep-sea diving resort of Hurghada. Ignazio and I have been tipped into its muffled beige luxury from the taxi that rescues us from the bus stop. Ten hours of a bumpy journey across the Arabian Desert mostly standing up has left us fragile with exhaustion. Propped at the main desk of the Hurghada oasis attending to the necessary formalities, I plunge both hands into the pockets of my jacket and empty their contents into the nearest rubbish bin, as if ridding myself of the chaos and clutter of the past day.

We only discover about the airline tickets the following day when, refreshed from a good night's sleep, we decide to organise ourselves for the home run to Cairo before flying back to Rome. When we stop panicking, we start to make phone calls: to both Italian and Australian embassies in Cairo, to Ignazio's parents in Florence – and incomprehensibly not to the airline company.

Our holiday funds have almost disappeared; we move out of the Sheraton and into the shabby Shedwan Hotel, where loose wires droop out of holes in the peeling bedroom wall, and slink several days later onto a Cairo-bound bus. At least we have the assurance of new airline tickets furnished by Ignazio's generous parents awaiting us at the airport. But meanwhile we have a day in Cairo, and so book into the Anglo Swiss Pension, a seedy hotel in a scruffy part of town. It is while we are sitting on the sagging bed biting into tomatoes and bread purchased earlier from a street stall that I have a sudden vision of the Sultan's Breakfast a fortnight previously. I had taken a photo of Ignazio sitting semi-naked on the giant bed of the Nile Hilton, framed by a line of golden pharaohs on the dark, wooden bedhead behind him. The bedlinen is crisp and white, the table pulled up to the bed has a gold linen cloth folded neatly over it, and from it Ignazio is spooning sugar into a cup from a silver bowl. Filling the table are more silver bowls, glassware, my carelessly crumpled napkin.

At least we have the tickets home.

Scalda piu l'amore che mille fuochi
Love burns more than a thousand fires

Back in Florence, the days shorten and I find myself in the kitchen preparing food and feeling nauseated beyond belief. All I want to eat are hard-boiled eggs. A pregnancy test is positive. The abortion, which we both feel unreservedly is the best decision, is efficient and forgettable. That same day I am back home, where Ignazio waits on me with devotion. There is no sense of loss or grieving; on the contrary, I am struck by a feeling of weightlessness and freedom. Crisis averted, we resume our placid cosiness.

By the time I met Raimondo, and then later his wife, they had been together for many years. Raimondo tells me he met his sweetheart Annamaria on the Ponte Vecchio, where he had set himself up with easel and paints. Being a painter is one of many skills: pianist-accordionist, polyglot, bon vivant, gardener, waiter, singer, cook and drinker. He is ten years older than Annamaria and, like Gianfranco, a boy from a small Umbrian village. Annamaria, on the contrary, comes from a good Florentine family. She has waist-length hair, enormous sorrowful eyes behind thick glasses, and a wardrobe of sensible Ferragamo shoes with flat heels. He works and lives in Florence, while she is a teacher of English to foreigners at the University of Perugia and lives in a little flat like an eyrie in one of the steep, narrow streets that drop away from Corso Vannucci. She speaks calm and exquisite English with a trace of an American accent, legacy of the years she spent at Harvard University acquiring her second or third degree.

The day Raimondo brought Annamaria to the restaurant to meet me we loved each other immediately. After the healing, soothing time I spent in the country following the Gianfranco breakup it was to Perugia I headed, boarding a bus to stay with Annamaria. In the week that I was there, we both gained five kilos due to nightly sessions of wine and cheese while I poured out my sorrow, usually lapsing gratefully into English as the evening wore on. Annamaria and Raimondo are my solid rocks, the most romantic story I know, two people so extraordinarily unalike, whose love withstands long absences and little infidelities. Perhaps it is precisely because they are such an odd couple that they accept so unblinkingly the oddness that is Ignazio and me.

Change seems to know when to strike and, as much as I feel that I control my life and determine my destiny, I see how I am just being buffeted along, tricked into placidness in order, perhaps, to be better prepared for the next upheaval. Unlikely we may be, but twelve months into the relationship Ignazio and I are very settled.

Then Raimondo does what he has long talked of doing: he buys a restaurant. The restaurant is in Perugia, so he can finally be with Annamaria all the time, and he offers a share in the business to Ignazio, who accepts. Not without hours of dialogue, discussion and debate with me, the upshot being that I too agree to leave the restaurant, where I have no further to go, and move to Perugia as well to seek work. I am conscious that there is much at stake in this decision, and that what is about to happen will alter the nature of my relationship with Ignazio, with whom lately I feel bothered, obscurely, by a score of details. He has changed so dramatically from the beautiful child that I lured into my clutches to a self-confident young man, smoking too many Marlboros and experimenting with facial hair. He goes to Perugia to set up the restaurant with Raimondo and to find us a little apartment in Via Deliziosa – I feel I could only love a place in a street so named. After a month, I have formally extricated myself from the restaurant and packed up our apartment in Via Ghibellina, storing boxes of books and summer clothes at Ignazio's parents' place. Then I catch a train to join my beloved.

Non tutte le ciambelle escono con il buco
Not every doughnut has a hole
(or, things don't always turn out as planned)

The steep, narrow streets in Perugia turn into tunnels for the wind and all the stone fortifying the town seems to contain and transmit the cold. Not quite as cold, however, as the previous winter, when the front page of *La Nazione* featured a photograph of nuns skiing through the streets of Rome, and when millions of hectares of precious grapes withered and died. Into Bar Sandri blow men in overcoats and women with scarves. Everyone is laughing and talking in high-pitched voices; the barista pours a stream of thick creamy milk into coffee cups lined along the bar. There is a complicated perfume of vanilla, hot pastries, grinding coffee and Fendi. Someone leaves with the wrong umbrella by mistake and rushes back in apologetically; everyone becomes suddenly involved in the incident and there are jocular cries to guard carefully one's own umbrella. My cappuccino has a heart on it where the steamed milk has been carefully poured, and from behind the bar the glamorous middle-aged woman with extraordinary glasses passes me a jam-filled brioche wrapped in a tiny serviette.

Perugia: closed stone city of walls and silences, muted women murmuring through passageways, a sudden muffled flutter of pigeons. And then the gaudy warmth of the piazza, lit up and twinkling with the beautiful people strolling and gesticulating and embracing, scarves and jackets swinging, boots clipping and shoulder bags sailing through the crowd. Sudden little streets as narrow as alleys dropping away from the main beat, twisting into cheese shops, bakeries pungent with vanilla and a tiny yellow stationer's cluttered with cards. The wood vendor is next door in his low-ceilinged garage with swarthy men who move soundlessly, piling wood into hessian bags. I climb the long, delirious streets until I reach Annamaria's apartment, where the fire in the kitchen is lit. We sit at her wooden table over wine, toasted slabs of bread with garlic and oil, creamy sheep's cheese and salad, and finish off with strong, good coffee.

In Via Deliziosa, I sprawl on the double bed filling in pieces of a 3,000-piece jigsaw puzzle, bored by too much sky. Ignazio bustles off early each morning and in the beginning returns mid-afternoon to spend several hours with me before heading back for the evening shift. I am half-heartedly looking for jobs, contemplating joining a gym, smoking thin joints of hashish in the evenings with introspective Talk Talk songs on the stereo. After a while, Ignazio begins to come home later and later in the afternoons. I am revisited by the Gianfranco experience – sick, lurching suspicion and jealousy – so one day I set off for the restaurant to look for him. Through the glass I see him sitting at one of the tables in the empty dining room, reading comics and stubbing out cigarettes. I creep back home and mention nothing.

All through that bleak isolated winter, I prickle with indecision. Despite the occasional company of Annamaria and Raimondo, I am not enjoying Perugia. I roam around the beautiful old town, drinking solitary *proseccos* in the lounges of fading elegant hotels, buying paper bags filled with assorted shortbreads from pastry shops, and writing long, introspective diary entries about my pointless life. I feel that I have taught Ignazio as much as I am capable. We make love uneventfully because I realise, too late, that in my challenge to educate him I have omitted to tell him how to best give me pleasure. I am reluctant to look for a job because of being so undecided. For the first time in four years, I begin to think seriously about returning to Australia; I change my mind every day.

Then Ignazio receives notice of his impending military service and everything is suddenly simplified. He will be away for one year – away from the restaurant, away from Perugia and, most importantly, away from me. This offers me the perfect reason to go back home, and from that vast objective distance sort out whether or not we have a future together. I buy a return ticket valid for twelve months and fly out of Rome several days before Valentine's Day. In the drawer where Ignazio keeps his underclothes, neatly folded, I have left a large chocolate heart and a note of love.

L'amore del soldato non dura un'ora:
dov' egli va, trova la sua signora
A soldier's love doesn't last an hour:
wherever he goes he finds his woman

For six months, Ignazio misses me terribly and loves me madly. Postcards arrive periodically – from Livorno, Piombino, Cecina – written in neat upper case and providing descriptions of typical soldier-days, noting how many months of military service remain. He mentions his fidelity often, invariably accompanied by comments regarding the extreme difficulty men have with the issue. Plans shift and alter; he has decided not to return to Perugia, which is a cold and boring town; Gianfranco is contemplating buying I' Che C'è C'è and would like Ignazio as a partner; he will join me in Australia.

In Sydney, I am selling advertising space for the Italian newspaper *La Fiamma*. I drive a turquoise Datsun 120Y between Leichhardt, where I work, and Balmain, where I inhabit a small flat. I am fat, gloomy and confused about what to do when the year is up; my letters to Ignazio become as rare as his are to me. There is a very large space where we have ceased communicating and then I hurl off a letter discussing my proposed return to Italy and expressing need for reassurance. I am so ambivalent about going back that it comes almost as a relief when Ignazio's breaking-off letter arrives. He acknowledges that he loves me still – the letter being, he comforts me, as difficult to write as it is to receive – but that at twenty years of age and on the verge of finishing his military service he realises his whole life spills before him. He no longer knows what he wants – he is ambitious, greedy, curious – and he has no desire any longer to settle down and raise a family with me, because what would happen in two or three years' time if he changed his mind and became tired of our relationship?

The letter is a relief because it puts an end to my confusion and decides the short term for me. I am utterly crushed by it at the same time. I fold it carefully back into its envelope, stunned by a sort of emptiness.

Book Two

1994
Spedaluzzo, near Florence

Se ne vanno gli amori, restano i dolori
Love departs, pain remains

Eight years pass. One day Gianfranco phones me. He and Ignazio have bought a restaurant in the Chianti district, thirty minutes out of Florence. It is opening in March. They would like me to come and work in the kitchen alongside Gianfranco as assistant chef, like the old days. Am I available?

How could I resist such symmetry? I am nearly forty years old, unmarried and childless. I am good at my job selling advertising space – now for a larger publication – and made reasonably satisfied by it. I teach Italian cooking at community colleges all over Sydney, live alone in a fashionable expensive suburb, have a wide circle of friends and spend most of my salary giving ambitious dinner parties. Occasional affairs peter out quickly. My monotonous, repetitive diaries maunder along under the fug of anxiety that I am becoming vacuous and inconsequential.

And so I decide on a six-month stint, spread over the European summer. I resign from my job and pack my life neatly into cardboard cartons and heavy-duty garbage bags, except for the overweight suitcase that accompanies me to the international airport. My accommodation will consist of rooms above the restaurant in the big, old building at the top of a hill where all of us will live. There will be Gianfranco (now divorced from Marie-Claire after producing two children) with his new younger woman, Cinzia, as well as Ignazio, a middle-aged kitchen hand called Vera… and me.

Gianfranco, over several phone calls, is characteristically enthusiastic, positive and vague about details, and, while I am aware how once again I go leaping into darkness, I know he will keep me safe.

Quandu si las 'a vecchia p'a nova,
sabe che lasa ma non sabe che trova
When you leave the old for the new, you know what you are leaving but not what you will find

Pino the butcher meets me at the railway station and drives me to the crossroads outside Florence where Gianfranco leans against a new Land Cruiser with his arms folded. We are heady and clumsy with excitement as we embrace. We talk the whole journey through countryside both familiar and strange, until we reach La Cantinetta. I am too high-pitched to sleep off the day and a half of travel; instead I familiarise myself with the restaurant's kitchen and throw together a cheesecake. Ignazio is badly shaven, pink-eyed and beautifully Ignazio – all grown up into a small man with the gentle beginnings of a paunch. Gianfranco's second wife, Cinzia, is vibrantly exotic and warmly gracious; Gianfranco is heavier and tamer. Much later, sitting over dinner, I look around at my new family, in particular at the shy, middle-aged woman called Vera with whom I am to initially share sleeping quarters. This I had not expected, although Gianfranco assures me the arrangement is temporary and within a week he will have knocked down more walls, erected cupboards and screens to create private rooms for both of us. For now we are piled higgledy-piggledy into large, cold rooms whose minimal furniture is either extraordinarily ugly or broken. There are flagged floors, wooden beamed ceilings from which naked light bulbs suspend in a lacy mesh of cobwebs, and doors that don't shut properly, preventing privacy. The restaurant has been officially open for several weeks, but business is sparse. Word has yet to spread that Gianfranco is now operating outside of Florence and, besides, it is the lingering tail end of winter.

I am unprepared for the sudden flurry of snow on my third afternoon. Sitting on my single bed opposite Vera, I look out of the window at flakes floating past and hear a crying wind that echoes my desolation. Before I fall into the habit of easily sleeping away the several hours between the day and evening shifts, and before I have reclaimed the luxury of a room to myself, I spend unsettled afternoons lying in bed pretending to be asleep in order to avoid conversation with the incessantly prattling Vera.

Vera sits upright on her bed, which is closest to the window, and stares out all afternoon at the opposite driveway and the cypress trees. Her husband is in hospital with lung cancer and her two married daughters have families of their own. She has come to work and live among complete strangers. She also has no idea that her chief function is washing up, instead of the cooking she was hoping to do, with which the blonde foreigner – whose back is turned so eloquently in her direction – has been bequeathed.

Gianfranco has made wooden chopping boards in various sizes upon which to serve our house speciality of *tagliata*. The result is spectacular. A slab of beef (the size depends on the number of people it must feed) is quickly cooked on the grill, then transferred to a chopping board, whereupon it is adorned with a series of diagonal slashes and topped with either rocket and shaved Parmesan, grilled garlicky ovals of zucchini, black truffles from Norcia or, in season, grilled whole porcini mushrooms. A drizzle of dressing, and out to the table it goes! The meat is sublime *Chianina*, rich red and meltingly tender.

I love La Cantinetta's menu and its blend of rustic fashionability. One of the most popular dishes that summer is *grigliata mista di verdura*, consisting of grilled capsicum, red onions, zucchini, aubergine, radicchio and tomatoes dressed with finely chopped parsley and garlic. The combination of colours glistening with golden oil is gorgeous. Then there is the battered-and-fried chicken with vegetables, which are served in a cone of stiff butcher's paper: golden nuggets of moist chicken and chunks of fennel, cauliflower, broccoli, artichokes and cardoons in a crisp light casing, spilling out onto a platter piled with potato chips.

Minestraia (pasta chef) once again, I am taught new and challenging sauces: duck to serve with fresh tagliatelle; wild boar with potato gnocchi; mutton with rigatoni; oxtail with fettuccine. Gianfranco shows me how to hold the duck over a gas flame until all the hairs are singed off, then to dismember it neatly with the cleaver. Even when it is the season of the boar we use wild boar that comes vacuum-packed from Hungary, local boar being invariably riddled with parasites.

Gianfranco, who considers the creation of desserts and cakes beneath him, had been whipping up batches of chocolate mousse from a packaged mix and experimenting with strawberry tiramisu. Briskly I take charge as he hoped I would and begin to bake in earnest. Within several days of arriving, however, I have one of my most important culinary lessons, which is the making of potato gnocchi.

Everyone has a version. Vera and I cluster around the two marble chopping boards. The potatoes, newly drained from their cooking water, are the gently steaming centrepiece. Neighbours, friends, suppliers and waiters, all talking at the same time, are forming the audience. Potatoes peeled before cooking, potatoes peeled after cooking, no eggs, yolks only, three eggs for every two kilograms of potatoes, fork prints obligatory – these are the vehement variations flying around the room.

Gianfranco, however, is the master, and his way will be The Way. He stands between us, his small knife briskly peeling the hot cooked potatoes, explaining that for minimal penetration of water great care must be taken when piercing the flesh to test for done-ness. Everything must be performed quickly. When all the potatoes are denuded, the area must be completely cleaned of all debris before stage two – the ricing – can begin. The potatoes are packed into a utensil resembling a giant garlic press and forced through the small holes; they become a mountain of snowy sieved potatoes. Flour is scattered onto the mountain and now Gianfranco's hands work the flour in, bit by bit, adding more as he goes. No eggs, absolutely no eggs at all, he dictates to the onlookers, eggs make the mixture stiff, the texture rubbery. He creates a smooth pillow of dough and urges us all to touch its firm silkiness. It is rolled out into sausage lengths; quickly his knife chops along the lengths at two-centimetre intervals, forming perfect little dumplings. These he drops into a pot of boiling salted water and cooks until they rise to the surface. The whole procedure looks fiddly but possible, and I had no idea then how many months of daily gnocchi-making it would take me to get them right, and for the tips of my fingers to become heat resistant.

It is fortunate that the first six weeks at the restaurant are so quiet. Before summer commences and before we are 'discovered', we all need time to shuffle into our respective roles and to turn this long-unused barn into a restaurant, and a destination worth the journey. We are not really in the middle of nowhere. There is a little village at the base of the hill whose bar I frequent for coffee at the end of my walks. The humming town of Greve is ten minutes away by car, and every ocular angle throws up vineyards, olive groves, blackberry bushes, forests and castles and monasteries and crumbling stone walls. In those first two grim, adjusting months, the enchantment of our surroundings is only caught in snatches and glimpses: shadows cast by poplars striping the white dirt track over the road, the spindly pencil pines in serried ranks out the window as the bus passes the Ugolino golf course.

I am mainly absorbed by the laying down of small new routines and the living with other people. After the first week, Gianfranco has set up a bedroom for Vera through the archway that leads from my room into the vast storage area. The poverty of her possessions makes me feel sad – the clutter of cosmetics, the paperback novel and a spectacles case on the wobbly chair beside her bed. At least we each have our own privacy, and begin to shyly eat meals together.

Ignazio has a girlfriend, a first-year university student with buck teeth and large breasts, who leans palely against the kitchen wall, too terrified to talk. He and I are not always easy together; there seems to be an entire universe around which we carefully step, although I often manage to leap across it with the sort of comment or joke I know he will respond to, and our eyes meet with brief warmth.

Until May, what diners we attract occupy the several small rooms inside the restaurant. Solid furniture, stiff floral linen with white over-cloths, lines of vintage Chiantis around the walls: Gianfranco and Ignazio have paid attention to every detail. In one of these rooms Vera and I sit eating grilled garlicky sausage with salad and the springy spongy bread I never manage to find in Australia, and cautiously permit each other peeks into our respective lives. Vera, like most Italian women, drinks little alcohol, although often – presumably under my pernicious influence, or perhaps in the spirit of our increasing intimacy – forgets to top up her wine glass with water and tosses back the contents with a sort of liberated recklessness, her white neck stretching. She is very discreet, and speaks of her husband, whom she visits at the hospital on her day off, in respectful though detached terms; more and more often I hear mentioned the name of her landlord, whom she refers to simply as 'Il Signore', referring vaguely to his many acts of kindness.

BOOK TWO

Behind the restaurant the two dining areas are being finished. The upper level consists of a roof upheld by pillars at whose bases lean terracotta pots of flowers, while tables look out across gently curving hills and vineyards and the small white dots of villages. A path leads away from this area, past an ancient stone olive press and towards another roofed enclosure filled with tables, chairs and hanging lampshades, and a bar-in-progress up one end into which Ignazio is pouring his builder's energies to a background of exuberantly thumping Brazilian music. Beyond the three-tiered fountain with the headless girl in green stone is Gianfranco's vegetable garden, flanked by fig trees. In the slowly thawing reluctant spring, there is little sign of the abundance to come.

My birthday coincides with a bicycle race, which is to finish at Chiocchio, the village at the bottom of the hill. We at the top of the hill expect to be busy, and prepare vast quantities of food, but are still overwhelmed by a day which pours in endless groups of people, on and on into the night, so that I keep forgetting that I have just turned the milestone of forty. At eleven o'clock that night, we finally draw breath; Gianfranco opens spumante and we sink gratefully into chairs. There are presents for me: a long, thin, wooden rolling pin inscribed with the signatures of Gianfranco, Cinzia and Ignazio, and a chopping knife.

That day signals the change we have been waiting for. It is May, and when I walk my early mornings are lighter and milder; we begin to acquire some regular customers. Signore Argento, the industrialist, telephones from his office several times a week to inform us that in half an hour's time he will be arriving with three guests for lunch. A bird of a man with a big moustache and expensive suits, he is invariably accompanied by glamorous Asian women. They all drink lots of mineral water and eat lightly, mostly salads or, the height of fashion that season, carpaccio. Over the phone Argento often requests *uno spaghettino* in a simple tomato sauce boosted by lots of chilli, which means I must put the water on the boil immediately to ensure that by the time he arrives there is no waiting. Carpaccio of beef is raw beef sliced paper-thin, but Argento begins to ask Gianfranco to sear the slices on the grill before sending them out to him with the simplicity of a cut lemon. The Asian women eat carpaccio of zucchini, carpaccio of tomato, carpaccio of mushroom – whatever thinly sliced vegetable Gianfranco has dreamed up and dressed evocatively, but they especially love the mixed grill of vegetables, which, unlike the Italians, they eat unaccompanied by bread. I catch myself gazing out the kitchen window at them, divining in that graceful wine-abstaining vegetarian asceticism the elegance of success.

La prova migliore dell'amore è la fiducia
The best proof of love is fidelity

Friends occasionally ring from Australia. One of them asks me, 'Are you happy? Are those boys looking after you?' And all I can reply is that, yes, in a mad sort of way I am happy and Gianfranco and Ignazio are sort of looking after me. The happiness mostly comes in brief flashes, and mostly in the early mornings on my walks, when the splendour of my

Grigliata mista di verdura
(Grilled vegetables)

2 aubergines
6 medium zucchini
2 red capsicum
4–6 small Spanish onions
3 radicchi
8 medium field mushrooms
6 Roma tomatoes
(Optional extras: asparagus, fennel, sweet potato)
1 bunch Continental parsley
2 fat cloves garlic
Salt and pepper
Olive oil

Wash all vegetables. Slice aubergines thinly. Slice zucchini thinly on the diagonal and cut deseeded capsicum into wedges. Peel and halve onions. Halve radicchi. Trim stalks from mushrooms and halve tomatoes lengthwise. Heat a ridged grill to moderate high, then grill all vegetables, brushing them with olive oil and seasoning as you go. Chop the parsley and garlic finely, mix, then stir in sufficient olive oil to form a loose paste. When all the vegetables are cooked, arrange on a large platter, drizzling over the garlic/parsley dressing while still warm.

surroundings spreads like a gift before me and I ask God to forgive my excesses and weaknesses.

I walk for an hour every morning, letting myself out of the building quietly and crossing the road before plunging downhill. Via Chiantigiana is the main highway between the two important towns of Florence and Siena but is just a narrow twisting road between vineyards and fields; I often have to leap into a field when two cars pass each other. (There is another occasional walk I do, through a silent, isolated forest studded with signs warning, 'Beware Vipers!') All summer Via Chiantigiana is busy with incessant traffic, but in spring it is largely empty and often shrouded in mists. I charge past naked vines and olive trees and the pretty little church of San Tommaso, almost concealed by creepers with its statuary and terracotta urns and peacocks. I greet farmers tending fields and scarved women hanging clothes on lines, and finally turn to retrace my steps at a little bridge before ending up at the Chiocchio bar for a cappuccino.

The household still sleeps as I let myself in and prepare for the day. Down in the silent kitchen I turn on lights, gas and oven and fill the huge pasta pot with water. Ignazio appears shortly afterwards, terse, bleary and hung over. Gianfranco is rarely seen before ten in the morning, when he blasts through the kitchen, makes himself an espresso, then retires to the outside toilet with the pink *Gazzetta dello Sport*. Vera silently unloads the dishwasher in her floral blouse and stretch slacks, with the smoke from the day's first cigarette coiling into her perm.

BOOK TWO

Towards the end of spring, the dining areas outside are completed and we have been discovered. One Thursday evening a group of Florentine professionals, friends of friends of Cinzia's parents, drive out, four couples as sleek and shiny as the cars in which they arrive. It is still too cool at night for outside dining, so they occupy one of the little rooms inside.

Whenever a good impression needs to be made, Gianfranco becomes short-tempered and pedantic; he crashes around the kitchen barking at everyone. He has already asked me to run up batches of tiny savoury shortbreads, twists of puff pastry baked with anchovies to be served with the pre-dinner drinks, and cocoa-dusted chocolate truffles to accompany coffee. Gianfranco bends over platters of antipasti, his forehead tight with concentration, his fingers softly arranging. The Florentine women all have dyed-blonde hair and hard, beautiful faces; they smoke endlessly and eat little. Baritone laughter bursts sporadically from their private dining room. We are to see these people and ever-increasing numbers of their glittery golden friends throughout the summer. Every time they come, there is the same frenzy of production in the kitchen, which is merely expected and never acknowledged. Over summer their suntanned limbs and breasts spill out of whites, creams and linens – they all holiday in Sardinia, the Isle of Giglio or, more exotically, the Maldives and Bali.

Six weeks seems to be the time it takes for a group of people to assume their own peculiar dynamic, and to shift into their own formation. Six weeks, too, for activities to be repeated enough times to turn into habits: the foundation of familiarity.

And so it is with our little group, pivoting, of course, around the central core, Gianfranco. Vera and I companionably arrange hard-boiled eggs and capers onto chunks of bread for our 11.00 a.m. *merenda*. Cinzia and I engage in long discussions about literature and, specifically, as Cinzia is an educated girl, English literature. Ignazio alternates between terse and flirtatious behaviour with me. As for Gianfranco, he and I have slipped back into being comfortable as we work silently together in the kitchen before service, or when we stand side by side at the stoves. Sometimes – and, as we become busier, these times increase – we move with such synchronicity that we are as graceful and as fluid as ballet dancers, dipping and weaving around each other without ever colliding. And yet his moodiness and volatility have not diminished with age – for the most part, at least, not directed at me, but at poor long-suffering Cinzia. '*Mi prende un nervoso,*' he barks. '*E poi m'incazz.*' – 'You make me irritable and then I get pissed off.'

I watch furtively as he teaches her how to tuck wine-glass stems into the webs of her fingers, to load the dishwasher, to carry hot plates all the way down the soft inner part of her arm. I see myself all those years ago, that pathetic desire to please him and to get it exactly right – and the impossibility of achieving either. He roars and bellows, or else subjects her to his famous ostracism while being warm and good-humoured to the rest of us. Much later on, when trust is established, Cinzia and I are able to build solidarity on this shared suffering.

Tempo, marito e figli vengono come pigli
Weather, husbands and sons
come as you take them

In our hideous communal bathroom – hideous and largely left uncleaned – there is a tumbling pile of comics beside the lavatory, an ashtray on a stand, and a bath from which one's nakedness is framed (if one is not careful) by the window overlooking the upper dining level. The washing machine belongs to Gianfranco and Cinzia, and so, once a week, after lunchtime service, I catch a blue SITA bus into Greve with my bag of laundry. In the early months I sit in the café in the central piazza in a shaft of watery sunlight with Amerigo Vespucci's statue straight ahead and colonnades all around, writing endless postcards over a beer. I collect my previous week's laundry from the laundrette and unfailingly feel pleasure at the way a carrier bag of crumpled malodorous sheets, towels and garments is transformed into a parcel resembling a stylish gift.

Down some undistinguished steps in the main piazza one enters the most exquisite bakery, a hole in the wall. There are always queues for the different loaves, rolls and cakes, but I often go in merely to absorb the aromas and visions. Sometimes I return from Greve with a wedge of fresh pecorino wrapped in wax-lined paper as beautifully as my laundry, to share with the others at dinner. A stuffed wild boar grins wickedly at the entrance of Falorni, considered one of the best butchers in Tuscany. German tourists clump around the racks of postcards; I move past them in the direction of the bus stop, clutching my parcel of laundry with the indifference of a local.

Up till the point Gianfranco decides to institute staff meals *before* instead of *after* service – a short-lived experiment – we eat together. The table is set in one of the rarely used end dining rooms until it becomes warm enough outside. We arrive in dribs and drabs, depending on any remaining customers. Gianfranco sits at the head, where his place is marked by a giant beer glass, from which he drinks his equal measures of wine and mineral water. We eat different things, although Cinzia tends to dine on whatever little delicacy Gianfranco has prepared. I slip effortlessly back into the soothing habit of eating the same thing nearly every night – an enormous salad to accompany the bread I love. It saves me thinking.

Occasionally, when he is at his most exuberant and magnanimous, Gianfranco suggests whipping up something for us all, and I eat one of Gianfranco's specials. These are always exquisite, taking the form of his version of beef carpaccio, or pizza dough stretched thin onto a baking tray and then strewn with rosemary, garlic and coarse salt before being cooked quickly, or pasta with eggplant sauce. Or sometimes it is a steak tartare, for which he bends earnestly over the chopping board with his big knife breaking down a piece of the leanest meat into fine mince.

His mood dictates the mood of the table. At his most cheerful, he sweeps us all up into the beam of his humour with witty stories, jokes and comments about customers.

BOOK TWO

But his ill temper sharpens the air with tension, which discourages conversation and hastens the meal to a joyless finish. The main reason why he decides to try out the notion of eating before service – I loathe it from the very beginning, finding that the meal and the two glasses of wine slow me down and dull me at a time when I most want to feel light, alert and empty – is because our late-night meals often tip over into the early hours of the morning, and generally we all drink too much. Grappa somehow finds its way onto our table amongst the debris of napery and breadcrumbs, and the smoking begins in earnest.

One night after service, I come across Vera on the landing that separates the stairs leading down to the restaurant and up to our bedrooms. She has a jacket slung over her arm and holds her handbag. Calmly she tells me about the phone call from the hospital bearing the news that her husband has died. Her daughter is coming to collect her. Gianfranco later describes how she crumpled against him when the phone call came; now she just seems like her sweet and practical self. We all understand that she is to be absent for several days only.

When ten days have passed, Cinzia reluctantly installed in front of the dishwasher, Vera's daughter rings to say that she will no longer be available to work for us. About six weeks later, she and her daughter return to collect her possessions – and this is the last we see of Vera.

We are now in June, with summer gloriously in train, and beginning to be extremely busy. Two enormous Sunday functions – one a communion, the other a wedding – have already taken place, and there are more booked to come. On

Salsa alla norma
(Aubergine sauce)

Wash and cube one large aubergine. Fry cubes in deep olive oil until golden all over, then drain on absorbent paper. Add to the final ten minutes of simmering basic tomato sauce and check seasoning. Tear fresh basil leaves into sauce and serve with pasta, passing freshly grated Parmesan separately.

these days we work through to the night, with maybe half an hour to sit down in the evening before hurling ourselves back into it.

Gianfranco tries out several surly Moroccan travellers, who are unsuccessful dishwashers. He snaps at Cinzia, argues with Ignazio, and is sarcastic towards me. One day I look at Cinzia and see how thin she has become, her face permanently anxious. She loads and unloads the dishwasher in her dreamy, graceful, inefficient way. We are already tired of the heavy hot days that are only just beginning. Privately, I am happy with my apple lattice pies and the tarts. I curl creamy custard into them, and then pile up an abundance of glazed berries.

Gianfranco returns from the Sant'Ambrogio markets in Florence with wooden boxes containing punnets of more types of berries than I ever knew existed. Deeper into the season I will use blackberries gathered from the bushes lining Via Chiantigiana.

When World Cup soccer season begins in June, Gianfranco moves our communal television down into the outside bar area. Every Friday and Saturday night for a month, matches are held between various countries and Gianfranco has made it perfectly plain that, as of 10.00 p.m., when the match begins, he will not be available in the kitchen; if customers want main meals, they must wait for half-time. He sits beside Ignazio in his stained apron and his clogs and they smoke in rapt concentration, periodically puncturing the thick air with howls of delight or derision, while male customers form small circles around them.

Crostata di frutta
(Fruit tart)

My perfect pastry
125 g butter
230 g (1 cup) plain flour
230 g (1 cup) self-raising flour
75 g (1/3 cup) caster sugar
1 egg yolk
3–5 tablespoons cold water

In a food processor (or by hand), work the cold diced butter into the flours until the mixture resembles breadcrumbs. Add sugar, then egg yolk beaten with water. The mixture should come together in a smooth ball – neither too wet nor too dry. Wrap in plastic film and chill for about an hour. Roll out and press into the removable base of a flan tin and up the sides (you won't need all the pastry). Trim pastry, then line with baking paper and fill with dried beans. Blind-bake in a 180°C (350°F, Gas mark 4) oven until pale and crisp. Remove and cool, discarding the baking paper and beans.

Custard filling

3 egg yolks
3 tablespoons caster sugar
3 dessertspoons plain flour
500 ml milk
Vanilla pod

Whisk together egg yolks, caster sugar and plain flour until thick and creamy. Bring milk and a vanilla pod to simmering point slowly over low heat. Remove vanilla pod then pour milk on to egg mixture, whisking well to blend. Return mixture to saucepan and, still whisking, keep stirring over gentle heat until thickened. Remove and cover surface with plastic film. When cool, dollop into cooled pastry shell and smooth.

Topping

Mixed berries
Apricot jam

Scatter mixed berries over the top to cover completely, then glaze with warmed and sieved apricot jam.

In spite of the harmony with which we work together, and a tamer side to his wildness I noticed from the beginning – and especially in spite of my determination all these years later not to be affected by his tantrums – Gianfranco remains a perpetual source of tension and mystery. One minute he is being so loathsome that I feel only contempt for him, and the next he has brought into the kitchen, cupped in his large hands, a sparrow from whose head blood gushes, which those same large hands tenderly wipe away. He calls me over to look, attempting to get the feeble little beak to sip some of the water he has trickled onto his palm. The tears that shoot into my eyes have less to do with the poor bird than with my compassion for this man with these crazy mood swings. Randomly occurring, they always manage to redeem him, to render him forgivable and lovable.

Non c'è amore senza amaro
You can't have love without bitterness

Tuesday is the day we close the restaurant. I invariably catch an early-morning bus into Florence and spend the day there. Gianfranco and Cinzia often travel to his village, while Ignazio tends to sleep until midday before linking up with friends. Sometimes he drives to hill towns like Montalcino and Pienza, returning with wheels of pecorino both fresh and aged.

One Wednesday morning Gianfranco erupts into the kitchen clutching a paper bag, which he thrusts at me, demanding that I open it. Even before I do, I recognise the smell, but am still unprepared for the vision of so many black Umbrian truffles, like nuggets of coal. Gianfranco's smile is wide enough to split.

We set up a trolley outside, in the top dining area among all the tables, and adorn it with the pecorino, the truffles, fat fresh *cappellacci* pasta stuffed like little pillows with ricotta and porcini mushrooms, rolls of salamis, *finocchiona* and pancetta. Also included are the two baked ricottas Gianfranco discovered in Greve – one studded with rocket and the other with strawberries – a whole prosciutto, a bottle of balsamic vinegar and several straw-wrapped flasks of Chianti. He arranges deep-green vine leaves around the platter of truffles, and on the bottom shelf of the trolley, beside a pile of white plates, he places one of my berry tarts, a glass bowl layered with creamy tiramisu and a splendid *torta della Nonna*.

No one eats inside any more, and most nights the sounds of ongoing parties drift into the kitchen, the guests staying later and later. We rarely dine together anymore, either – I usually finish work well before everyone else, so I carry my large bowl of salad, bread basket and wine out to a vacated table to luxuriate in the bliss of finally sitting down, observing other tables, and eating and drinking my way through a soft, warm night.

There occur the occasional days off when, in an anti-Florence state of mind, I catch a bus somewhere, anywhere – a randomly plucked village in Chianti.

One of the first lessons Gianfranco taught me was about Gallo Nero and the Chianti Classico wine zone. This was in

Torta della Nonna
(Grandmother's tart)

Pastry
350 g plain flour
1 1/2 teaspoons baking powder
75 g sugar
150 g cold butter, cubed
1 egg, plus 1 egg yolk, beaten

Whizz in a food processor until it comes together in a smooth ball. Wrap in plastic film and chill while you make the filling. Preheat oven to 175°C (340°F, Gas mark 4).

Filling

600 ml milk
1/2 vanilla pod
2 eggs, plus 1 egg yolk, beaten
75 g caster sugar
65 g plain flour, sifted
75 g ground almonds
Slivered almonds and pine nuts
Milk for glazing
Icing sugar mixture

Heat milk with the vanilla pod to boiling point. In a
separate bowl, beat eggs and sugar until thick and pale,
and whisk in flour. Remove vanilla pod from milk, scrape
out seeds and reserve. Whisk while trickling milk into eggs.
Pour mixture into saucepan and, over a moderately high
heat, cook until thickened, stirring constantly with whisk.
Remove from heat and beat in ground almonds and vanilla
seeds. Cover with plastic film and set aside to cool.
Roll out the pastry and press into a greased flan tin. Blind-bake
until crisp – around 10 minutes in a moderately hot oven. Cool,
then fill with custard filling. Scatter over lots of toasted slivered
almonds and pine nuts, then dredge thickly with icing sugar.

the early days at the restaurant where we met and where I would type up the lists of wines, enchanted by the poetry of their names. That first restaurant was a celebration of Chianti wines, and its cellars – three, vast, low-ceilinged rooms at the back of the dining area – were crammed with endless bottles laid horizontally in wooden racks depicting every type, year and region. It was a collector's dream. I learned that the Chianti Classico zone covers about 7,000 hectares between Florence and Siena; that the black rooster (*gallo nero*) appearing on the neck labels of many Chianti Classico wines is the symbol of the Consorzio del Vino Chianti Classico, a foundation of producers in the region whose aim is to promote the wines, improve their quality and prevent wine fraud; and that the wine must be produced with a minimum of eighty per cent Sangiovese grapes.

And so, to bump along roads which wind through valleys and hills gazing out the bus window at these familiar names feels like finding myself the character in a book I have read, as well as constituting a journey through towns, villages and vineyards that compose a list of Chiantis I have drunk: Impruneta, Radda, Castellina, Querciabella, Badia a Passignano, on and on through postcard countryside. Until, suddenly, I am inspired to alight. At Panzano, there is just one main road leading through a medieval town which was originally an entire castle among vineyards. It always amazes me that, despite the ongoing fashionability of Tuscany, there are so many villages where you may be the only visitor browsing in shop windows, having an espresso in a bar, taking photographs of church façades.

One afternoon Ignazio surprises me by inviting me to accompany him on one of his trips to Montalcino, famous for its Brunello wine. His car winds up through vineyards until we reach the top of the hill. From the fortress the valleys below are bathed in pale gold. We sit outside at a little table and drink wine the colour of translucent cherries, our conversation innocuous and comfortable, then climb more stepped and narrow streets for more views and, in another bar, more Brunello tastings from enormous glasses.

Another day I choose Il Ferrone in order to visit the terracotta factories I have often heard mentioned; on yet another, Piero, my old boss from I' Che C'è C'è, arrives to take me out. My arms encircle his waist for one of our motorcycle jaunts up to Montefioralle, a fortified village within medieval walls so lovely I fantasise, briefly, about living there. Cobbled streets and low doorways and tiny windows belong to another century; it is only the presence of several posters up on a wall that suggests the present. From a small plain menu we order crispy *fettunta* (grilled bread rubbed with garlic and drizzled with olive oil), spaghetti with spicy wild boar sauce and moist grilled chicken with zucchini. Even in these timeless little hamlets there will always be at least one chic boutique selling exquisite garments neatly folded on shelves: smart linen trousers, delicate woollen knits, silky sensuous blouses I dare not disturb with my clumsy, grubby fingers.

I am asked to write an article about panettone for a prominent Australian food magazine's Christmas issue. On several Tuesdays I spend time at my favourite Florentine bookshop, the Libreria Edison in the Piazza della Repubblica, where I position myself in front of the cookery section and learn about this traditional Christmas fruitcake. The article must be written by the end of July and enclose a workable recipe.

This bothers me somewhat, because I have never known anyone who has actually made this cake, a cake famous for being labour-intensive and complicated. Once the piece has been written, Gianfranco and I set about the task of creation. We quickly discover how no one in his right mind would ever consider making panettone so unseasonably in the middle of summer, what with the twenty minutes of kneading the dough required. We share these twenty minutes with perspiration coursing down our faces as we grimly work through a heatwave. The whole process takes between nine and twelve hours, although most of this is yeast- and dough-rising time. Just before midnight I remove the panettone from the oven to find it is a spectacular failure. It has barely risen to the top of the special, high-sided tin I have purchased for it; moreover, it is slightly burnt! My disappointment is fractionally less intense than my sense of panic.

We try again the next day using a slightly different recipe from a magazine. This time I am so determined to succeed that I do not heed the discomfort. The vision of that puffy golden dome and the perfume of the vanilla sweetening the air come as a great victory at the end of the night. I send the article off several days later, accompanied by some proud photos, but somehow cannot bring myself to even taste the thing, which has ceased to be food.

Instead of museums and art galleries on my day off, I hang around shops. The six days spent boxed up at Spedaluzzo with neither need nor time to spend my hard-earned lire result in a desire almost physical to do so each Tuesday when I descend upon Florence. My list of items such as cotton balls and talcum powder is briskly attended to in stores like UPIM and Standa, after which I am free to roam, dipping into small side streets and across bridges, alternating between dusty forgotten pockets and expensive fashionable ones.

My camera accompanies me, slung over my shoulder alongside my handbag strap. I take photographs of bakeries and cheese shops, German tourists eating *gelato*, a circlet of old men standing chatting outside a bar, a sudden glimpse through complicated wrought-iron gates of inner courtyards. Pictures snap of bloodless mannequins in designer-shop windows, and a gypsy woman sitting cross-legged in front of a Brunelleschi door, her head bowed over a white lamb in the afternoon shade of the Duomo. In the Boboli Gardens, the camera captures a timeless moment, when before me like a painting I am offered the tableau of a boy in a bath to escape the heat. A long, lean youth has climbed into an Etruscan bath on a mound of pebbles in a corner of coolness, his head thrown back against the green-grey stone.

I see the coat of my dreams in a slick minimalist shop off Via de' Tornabuoni. It is black ankle-length pure wool, soft as moss, lined with satin and double-breasted. With its slightly padded shoulders and nipped-in waist, it instantly transforms me into a small blonde Anna Karenina. It costs a month's salary and I force myself to consider the impulse over a beer at Paskowski's. This, the beer, is always part of the ritual and, in spite of the haughty waiters in white jackets who bring tiny dishes of salted biscuits to accompany my drink, the black-toothed woman in charge of the toilets always greets me warmly. I extract postcards of Tuscan countryside from a brown paper bag and spend the next forty minutes engrossed in writing on the backs of them. Then I quickly march off to the coat shop, suddenly terrified that my coat is already gone, and when I discover it still there I immediately reserve it. Naturally.

Alvaro comes to save us, a short black Florentine with darting, dancing black eyes with a gently sloping paunch that hides the waistband of his apron. He loads and unloads the dishwasher with energy, washes sinkfuls of lettuces, mushrooms and leeks, springs sycophantically into the role of Gianfranco's sidekick and becomes my new friend. He is full of jokes, winks and songs; the corners of his mouth are used to store cigarettes and the restless beginnings of funny stories. I love him more when I discover his annual custom of participating in Calcio in Costume: a traditional Florentine procession of soccer teams dressed in medieval costume. He drinks too much, calls me 'Vickovski', and occupies the little alcove Vera used to inhabit. He becomes a buffer for Gianfranco's moods and tantrums and Ignazio's surly silences. I smell his cigarette smoke in the darkness from the room I have made cluttered and snug, through whose window late into the night I continue to hear sounds of groups leaving the restaurant, car doors slamming and choruses of *'buona notte'*.

On my days off in Florence, I sometimes cut my way through the crowds congesting the Ponte Vecchio to visit Lidia in her leather shop. Lidia is blonde, a translucent-skinned Sussex girl who has been living in Florence for the past twenty years – she is almost Italian. The partner of Fabio, our jack of all trades, she was first introduced to me long ago when I was Gianfranco's girlfriend, but it is really only now that we have cultivated a friendship of sorts. She manages the elegant, expensive boutique for a Florentine who is largely absent, and if I arrive too early for her to take her break I observe her with customers. With Italians she slips easily into relaxed idiomatic Tuscan; with the tourists she is polite and English. Then she is locking the door and clipping in her smart, heeled boots over the bridge with me, heading to a favourite bar for lunch.

We sit in the cool interior and talk. I usually begin, because I must spill out the past six days of Spedaluzzo to a sympathetic Anglo-Saxon female who speaks the same language – who, moreover, is familiar with the cast of characters whose latest exasperating, upsetting or bewildering behaviour I am now describing. There is such a comfort for me in her calm, resigned presence, in the way she lightly rests the spout of the ceramic teapot against her curled fingers as she pours, in her prolonged understanding nods and murmurs of 'I know, I know'. I tell her about the latest batch of eleven-and-a-half-hour working days, and about the tantrum that Gianfranco threw after I accidentally knocked over two containers of sauce in the refrigerator – admittedly on to his newly cleaned floor – and the way he started seizing things from the fridge and demanding to know why I needed four lots of cream and two separate packages of pancetta, before hurling them to the ground. How I then flounced out of the kitchen and up to the sanctuary of my bedroom.

I describe how my jeans are acquiring that strained level of discomfort because of all the bread and cheese and wine I so chronically consume. I relate the cruel comments Gianfranco made about my latest haircut, and how distressingly distant Ignazio is. How cloistered and claustrophobic it becomes, quickly, between all of us working and living there together. How when Gianfranco challenged me as to why I don't dream up new pasta sauces to have as weekly specials I explained that the few times I did he would laugh and tell me, 'We Italians don't eat that sort of thing,' but then later would ask me to think up an interesting way to bake the round zucchini he had just brought back from the markets. So, just the usual mixture of coldness and kindness.

Lidia listens with unswerving patience, making soothing noises as she forks cake into her lipsticked mouth. Because I have worked myself up, I tell her how easy it is to lose sight of the fact that couth, civilised, intelligent life pulsates beyond the small portal of La Cantinetta. Then I stop talking, sit back and allow her to take over. Even though she has not been able to resolve any of my frustrations and worries, the mere act of pouring them all out has rendered them manageable, even a little humorous.

Meanwhile, Lidia gratefully accepts the opportunity to unburden herself. I hear the next instalment in the tale of the house renovations, which seem to have been going on interminably. It is a nightmare. She is worn down by the chaos in which they live; Fabio is so fantastically busy helping other people with their projects that he has little time to spare for their own. And then, of course, she must cook and clean and do all the servile things expected of Italian women, in spite of the long hours she works in the shop. I know she loves Fabio, but sometimes it is hard to glimpse affection through the litany of complaints against him. Sometimes we find ourselves lapsing back into Italian when it seems that the matching English expression does not sufficiently convey the sense or the sentiment. Then we catch ourselves, and laugh. Afterwards, outside the bar, we wrap our arms around each other before separating, and I know that for her, as for me, the feeling of being fortified will remain for a long time. It will get us through.

*Chi mangia e non invita, possa
strozzarsi con ogni mollica*
He who eats alone and invites no one
may choke with every crumb

Even knowing that my time here is both finite (home before it becomes seriously cold, home for Christmas) and instructional does not prevent regular assaults of loneliness. 'You exclude yourself,' Gianfranco tells me, referring to my tendency in a late-night post-work group to head off to bed well before anyone else, to mostly dine alone, to submerge into the pages of a novel while all around me a jovial, noisy conversation takes place. The fact is that, older this time round, I find myself less amiably tolerant of traits I once found so charming. As I am no longer anyone's girlfriend, I am able to be my resolute Australian self, refusing (at least in spirit) to bow to the essentially chauvinistic character around me. I am outraged when I learn how Gianfranco expects Cinzia and me to clean the awful bathroom, despite the fact that we all work the same long hours; I am appalled rather than amused when I witness evidence of marital infidelity on the part of husbands, even though I know most wives take it for granted.

I find myself irritated by the facility for spontaneity and the relative, dubious, subjective concept of 'time'. I always used to love the looseness with which rules are applied, an almost inability to take anything truly seriously, and yet now am often frustrated by it. The passion poured into the most trivial of emotions, experience or anecdote at times exhausts me, and I find myself longing for the laconic texture of Australian life. Six days of the week boxed inside that big old hilltop building – with its fading Spedaluzzo sign on the side wall, the heavy green gates chained shut and padlocked each night – make for an odd existence. Invariably, each Tuesday night, when I have caught the blue bus back from Florence, I sit for a couple of hours over a letter to sisters or friends in which the usual self-absorbed scrutiny of my inner life goes on.

In fact, I see how my reaction is a function not only of my upbringing and culture, but perhaps more significantly of my own insecurities. Unpredictability always throws me out; unpunctuality and behaviour outside of expectation leave me thin-lipped with disapproval. And yet, all those years ago, younger and more malleable, I was charmed by the ease with which one's path could be diverted, and it seemed that if I stayed long enough in Italy I too might become spontaneous.

I used to love the way, en route to an appointment, Gianfranco and I would bump into someone we knew, and immediately be bundled off to the nearest bar for a coffee. Everyone operated like this, so it was perfectly acceptable to be late. It is a talent for living, and living fully for the moment, involving oneself completely in the landscape of life. In the face of it, I see how pinched and deliberate my own life is – and yet I am incapable of changing.

A chi trascura il poco mancherà pane e fuoco
Be grateful for what you have

Piero, my old boss from I' Che C'è C'è, putters up the hill on his motorbike and parks it on the gravel next to the garbage skips. I would never have imagined Piero as a biker – he is such a refined man – and yet his fingers are self-assured as he tightens the strap of the second helmet under my chin and kicks the machine into life. He comes to my rescue, on occasional weekday afternoons, and bears me off to villages and hill towns to look at castles and taste wines and attend markets and little local festivals, or *sagre*, which take place throughout the year in celebration of mushrooms or wild boar or a type of flower. Dear Piero is unchanged after all these years, though no longer running a restaurant, but throwing his energies instead into taking groups of tourists to vineyards and educating them about wines.

I lean with Piero around bends and curves as we twist our way up to hill towns enclosed by walls; Piero's stomach is all hard muscle. At Il Palagio vineyard in Castellina in Chianti we are enchanted by the little castle that perches in its grounds. Clicking our way across the intricately tiled inner courtyard, we find the pretty chapel with its mosaic walls, its slender soulful Madonna and its violent canvases depicting slaughter.

We bump along unsealed tracks until we reach a low, flat building in the middle of a homely farmyard. Inside the building, Danish girls with fiercely ruddy cheeks and white shower caps scrub down endless expanses of stainless steel at the end of the ricotta-making shift. Domes of snowy cheeses imperceptibly quiver in neat lines. At the lily *sagra* (festival), we stand before an antique olive press, eating sticky fried pastries, while Piero explains to me all the stages of olive oil production. He shouts back to me, riding pillion, an amusing story about a mushroom hunt with friends in nearby woods, where unplanned psychedelic experiences occurred, and I laugh into the laundry fragrance of his shirt.

These outings return me to a sense of where I am and who I am, expanding my world with possibilities. I invariably come back resolving to pack more into my days here, but, unless Piero visits, resettle into the habitual groove.

July and August are fantastically hot, the outside temperature in the high thirties and the kitchen worse.

Fortunately, during the day we are not busy, but in the evenings we run. Whereas I am used to making batches of tiramisu on a twice-weekly basis, I now find myself needing to do so every day. A small fan whirrs asthmatically beside me all night long in the little room I have come to think of, for all its eccentricities, as a haven.

One Saturday night around the middle of August, Cinzia stands in the corridor screaming that she needs to go to hospital for tranquillisers. Gianfranco, in a voice like ice, orders her to go upstairs to bed. I sit beside her as she sobs and heaves, and I say soothing, meaningless things until she becomes calm.

After Cinzia's breakdown, Gianfranco decides we all need a break, to tie in with the annual national midsummer holiday, Ferragosto. Incredibly, the cocktail of heat and intense working conditions has made Gianfranco contrarily good-humoured and cheerful – presumably, the success of the restaurant is contributing as well – and he and I fire along together beautifully. Even Ignazio (whose girlfriend, I realise, I dislike precisely because she possesses three features I lack – namely, youth, beauty and slenderness) behaves with less ambivalence, and more friendliness, towards me.

One night at five to midnight, I find myself sitting in bed surveying my room – plunged into shadow and lit by one tiny bedside lamp – with pleasure. Today I made forty-two crêpes and two cheesecakes, one flourless chocolate cake and a double carrot cake, a batch of *biscotti di Prato*, savoury *biscottini*, *salsa di guanciale* and *salsa ghiotta*.

Through pinched, tired eyes I look at the luxuriant plant in the tiny alcove below the window, my desk cluttered with books, letters, photos, pens, envelopes and diaries. There's my handbag and a flask of Chianti propping up mail. This is one of the rare times I feel a quiet happiness because, despite having failed my last few attempts at dieting, I am beginning to think I will drop the notion of being a tiny size 8 and relax into just being me. Now that would be progress.

In August, everyone heads to either the seaside or the mountains. Florence is almost deserted, with most businesses closed behind the ubiquitous green shutters.

Gianfranco and Cinzia leave for their days off. They have decided to close the restaurant for five days to go to the Isle of Giglio, where Cinzia's parents own a house. Ignazio heads off to Yugoslavia with a group of mates and I elect to stay behind at Spedaluzzo in luxurious solitude.

I read and walk in the afternoons instead of early mornings. I write lots of letters, and at night watch dreadful variety programmes on television as I spoon *gelato* into my mouth.

Mangia che ti passa
Eat and you will feel better

For most of that intensely hot summer, both the hot water system and the toilet in our bathroom are out of order. Essential functions and services breaking down is a facet of everyday life taken for granted in this battered ancient country, as presumably it is in all other countries not 'new' like Australia – the general response is philosophical.

Since my first time in Italy, I have experienced on innumerable occasions the disappearance of water for no apparent reason. The time it occurred on an extremely busy night at the first restaurant is the most memorable. Crates of mineral water had to be emptied into the enormous pasta pot; into the sink, for washing up; over our hands, for regular hand-washing. The chaos was extraordinary, and yet outside the kitchen the customers calmly enjoyed their meals without the slightest suspicion. In the Via Ghibellina flat shared with Ignazio, the shower water once stopped just as I was about to rinse off the foamy white conditioner from my hair. Fortunately, we had a barber shop directly below us into which I could drip so I could finish the job. On the Isle of Elba, it happened so frequently that I became adept at showering with the aid of bottles of mineral water – lathering up, rinsing off – and, on the nights I needed to wash my hair, would require a store of eight bottles do so effectively.

After two months, Fabio, our jack of all trades – a massive man whose large, loose jeans hang low around his hips, whose Florentine accent is almost incomprehensibly thick, whose soul is infinitely gentle – arrives to bring salvation. Until then, the cold baths I have been sinking into every afternoon in the heat are all I desire, and flinging a bucket of water down the toilet to flush away the contents seems as efficient a method as any. Once Fabio has left, all he has fixed we experience as absolute luxuries; this sense of luxury and privilege and ease of life remains with us for a long time afterwards.

There is an unexpected phone call from Emba – beloved mother-figure from I' Che C'è C'è – who has invited Piero and me to her place on a day off but not until late afternoon, allowing me to first visit the Valentino exhibition at the Accademia. I am up even earlier than usual to catch the bus into Florence, which deposits me behind the Santa Maria Novella station a little before nine o'clock. I spend an entrancing two hours in the lofty gallery, where David has been surrounded by shop dummies attired in red evening gowns falling to the floor in drapes and folds, pleats and swirls; most of them have been loaned, for the purposes of the exhibition, by movie stars like Sharon Stone and Glenn Close, according to tiny plaques beside each one. The drama of contrast, making that sublime statue whose imitations and reproductions are ubiquitous throughout the city the naked centrepiece for a room of red-gowned headless women, is both audacious and ingenious. Or perhaps just quintessentially Italian... I am still filled with the wonder of it when the bus tips me out at Spedaluzzo, so that shortly afterwards, when Piero arrives, it is all I can breathlessly talk about.

Piero is excited for other reasons: he has a brand-new BMW, larger than the previous motorcycle, and is eager to roar back toward Florence, to where Emba and her family live.

It is to be the first time I have seen her in years and years, but she is exactly as I remember her: round and soft and sweet and warm, if a little greyer. Ever since I' Che C'è C'è days, she and Piero have called me *'coniglietta'*, or 'little rabbit' – and thus I am called all that very long afternoon-into-evening. The apartment she shares with her gentle silent husband, two bossy grown-up daughters and Maurizio – who, thinner than before, makes a brief appearance – has as its hub a small kitchen around whose table we settle, all talking over the top of each other. Even though Emba no longer works in restaurants, food and cooking remain her great joys, and so, over glasses of the superior expensive spumante Piero has supplied, these largely constitute our conversation. And then the table is being set and the dishes brought out. There is *buristo*, the Sienese equivalent of *boudin*, or blood sausage, which Emba has sliced thinly, dipped in flour and fried in a little oil. We eat it with bread, like pâté. *Pecorino al tartufo* is fresh pecorino seamed with black truffles and is both earthy and creamy. The local green olives inspire Piero – who has become an expert in olives and grapes while taking group tours through vineyards – to tell us that green olives make the best extra virgin olive oil because of their asperity and their greenness, although obviously their yield is always much lower than that of the fully ripe, juicy black ones. There is a platter of rape, deep green leaves like spinach, which Emba has simmered in olive oil, garlic and a little *brodo* (chicken stock).

I love most the pasta dish, with Emba's own *salsa erbe*, or herb sauce, which she has folded through fresh tagliatelle. In between mouthfuls, I copy down the recipe on the torn-off sheet of a pharmaceutical company notepad.

All through the afternoon and the evening, and until it becomes dark, we eat and talk and laugh and pose for photos. I am exhausted – the day has been almost too rich. And out come Emba's sticky orange biscuits which she made

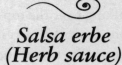

Salsa erbe
(Herb sauce)

*4 leeks, white part only, cleaned
thoroughly and chopped coarsely
4 sticks celery, chopped roughly
1/2 cup rosemary leaves
1 bunch fresh sage, roughly chopped
Olive oil
2 heaped teaspoons dried tarragon
2 heaped teaspoons dried marjoram
3 fat cloves garlic, finely chopped
1/2 bunch continental parsley, finely chopped
Salt and pepper
Cream*

*In a food processor, whizz together leeks, celery, rosemary
and sage, until they form a paste. Heat olive oil in a pan
and sauté vegetables on moderate heat, stirring frequently,
until softened – about 12 to 15 minutes. Add dried herbs
and about 2 1/2 to 3 cups water. Bring to the boil, then
simmer slowly until reduced and fairly dense – up to 30
minutes. Season with salt and pepper, and stir through garlic
and parsley. Simmer another 5 minutes. To serve, slosh
in a little cream. Simmer for several minutes, then toss in
the cooked, drained pasta, coating thoroughly over a high
heat. (For salsa ai'che c'è c'è, combine equal parts salsa erbe
with basic tomato sauce, add cream, check seasoning and
bring to a simmer before adding cooked, drained pasta.)*

especially for her small Australian rabbit – and the ones we do not eat she bundles up for me to take home, even though, sated beyond comfort, I have vowed never to eat again.

I am relieved when Piero eventually announces that we must leave; I have almost depleted my store of brightness. The fact that for half a day, however, I have been called a *coniglietta* has had the effect – like a tonic – of dispelling my usual self-regard, that of a middle-aged woman (*di una certa eta* – of a certain age) blundering thickly through the days, creating the occasional miracle of a dessert but mostly making no difference at all in the grand scheme of things. We roar off, Piero and I, into the night, swathed separately and together in the love and generosity of a glorious woman.

Once Ferragosto is over, summer starts to slide away. The groups of glittering golden Florentines – the thin, bosomy women dressed in white, the beautiful ponytailed men dangling linen jackets from one shoulder – are suddenly no longer there to transform Saturday nights into lavish garden parties.

Angelo the mushroom man arrives with crate after crate of porcini mushrooms brought in from Romania and Hungary – it is still too soon for local supply – haggling endlessly with Gianfranco over the price. Porcini feature in risottos, on crostini, as pasta sauces, sliced paper-thin on top of carpaccio, grilled whole, studded with garlic and, of course, cresting Gianfranco's famous *tagliate*.

After he finishes unloading the crates from his truck, Angelo comes into the kitchen and stands so close to me that I can hear the private rumblings of his stomach. The second time he comes to us, he thrusts me up against the sink with his groin and tells me how much he likes me; twenty-five years of untrustworthy men behind me enable me to retort that, since we have never had a conversation, I find it difficult to believe. Nonetheless, his attentions are flattering – I also suspect his untrustworthiness is part of his charm. He is tall and skinny with a moustache that droops, baggy eyes and a husky cigarette voice; his energy and self-confidence make me look forward to his visits, despite Gianfranco's words of caution. Of course he is married, a minor detail which fails to prevent him from asking me out on a date. The date – a drink somewhere, some night, after I have finished work – is mentioned, but never takes place.

Past experience never managed to teach me how to distinguish loneliness from lust. It is Ignazio, for all his wariness, who satisfies the latter on two occasions. We end up in bed together – the first time at his initiation and the second at mine – in the early months of La Cantinetta. Both times are as sweetly, easily, excitingly familiar as love-making with ex-lovers always is, although the second occasion concludes with a serious discussion about his girlfriend Milena, in which we surprise ourselves by agreeing like grown-ups that it isn't really fair on her and that we should desist. Our eyes pointedly refuse to meet when we sit over dinner in her company the following evening. Somehow, this seals the decision.

Several sets of friends visit me over the summer, but the most significant of them are Valerie and Douglas Hammerfield, a couple I had met at a cooking class in Sydney. On the brink of their trip to Tuscany, Valerie had been having her hair styled in a Balmain salon where she happened to read an article about Villa Vignamaggio, the setting for Kenneth Branagh's film version of *Much Ado About Nothing*. This is where they are staying, they tell me breathlessly when they arrive at La Cantinetta for lunch one day. Inspired by its beauty, they have hit upon the idea of bringing small groups of people over from Australia for week-long residential cooking courses there. Would I be interested in the position of cooking teacher?

Some months previously, Ignazio took me to the Villa Vignamaggio. It is one of the smaller estates, comprising a vineyard and olive groves, and its wines are considered to be superior. Various myths surround the villa. One is that Mona Lisa was born there; another is that it has a system of underground caves in which espionage took place during the last war, but one truth is its glorious beauty. For Branagh's film, it was repainted a rosy pink and now sits in its new colour among cool walls of cypress, a huge ornamental garden, lemon trees in giant urns, hedges and shrubbery clipped into topiaries.

Valerie's idea is that, towards late October, when I finish at La Cantinetta, we move into the villa in readiness for the group she will hopefully muster together upon her return to Australia. In the meantime, I am to prepare a week's worth of cooking classes, visits to vineyards, cheese factories and hill towns, and other activities I consider worth including. It seems like a wildly ambitious scheme, even when she assures me that she has already discussed it with the villa's manager. I decide to see how Valerie fares back in Australia before drawing up a programme, although I do talk about it with Gianfranco, who is enthusiastic and promises to help me with the cooking class menus.

My October walks are punctuated by the sounds of rifle shots of the hunting season. Men in camouflage become a common sight at that hour, and my mother writes urging me not to let myself be mistaken for a wild boar. Our menu has various game dishes on it – Gianfranco's casserole of pheasant with pancetta is particularly glorious – and he himself darts off at intervals to go hunting with friends. Now it has turned cool, business has slowed to a point where I am bored and longing for it all to be over; I find myself counting down the time remaining, feeling the absence of home and family and friends more acutely than ever. I sit in my little spot by the stoves, my head lowered purposefully over novel after novel, sipping surreptitious glasses of Chianti and chewing chunks of tangy Parmesan, while all around me the others clown, tell amusing anecdotes, have earnest discussions about sport and watch the little television we have propped up at the end of the workbench.

One of my jobs each evening is to chop handfuls of potatoes and throw them into a baking dish with fresh rosemary, garlic cloves and olive oil, and then roast them until they are crisply golden on the outside and creamy in the middle. I pick at them all night, guilty, furtive nibbling with my mouth barely moving, my thighs encased in larger looser trousers, ever-spreading. (I am already planning a grim campaign of Jenny Craig diet and daily vigorous swimming the minute I arrive back in Australia.)

Valerie confirms that eight people are booked into the Villa Vignamaggio cooking week, and I abandon my ritual of afternoon letter-writing to concentrate instead on organising the programme. Piero has promised to help, as well, offering to escort the group on a day trip to Siena with lunch thrown in at one of his favourite restaurants, and to hold a wine-and-cheese-tasting session another evening. I begin to post parcels of personal belongings back home, and suddenly it is my last week at La Cantinetta and I am packing up the contents of my spartan little room and preparing to leave.

Finchè c'è vita c'è speranza
Where there's life there is hope

'Much Ado About Chianti' begins with torrents of rain beating down the sides of the hired minivan as we drive to Florence airport to pick up our group. Blessedly the rain disappears overnight, leaving a cool, dry week for our ramblings.

Each day there is a cooking class either in the morning or the afternoon, held in a tiny galley-like kitchen attached to the guests' dining area. Gnocchi, pasta sauces, casseroles and desserts are somehow produced around a domestic electric stove, which dies on the second last day, so that we are forced to rush the *castagnaccia* pressed into its round tin over to the manager's private apartment, where her oven obligingly cooks it for us. (It is still pronounced too odd for enjoyment, this flat, rubbery cake made from chestnuts and seasoned with rosemary.) The rest of the time we are in and out of the minivan, visiting Greve markets, ceramic factories, vineyards, castles, a ricotta factory, and beautiful Siena, where Piero herds us into Osteria le Logge for buttery strands of fresh tagliatelle bathed in *ovoli* mushroom sauce, then later, an *enoteca* to sip *Asti spumante* in the thin afternoon sun.

Valerie, Douglas and I share one of the apartments at the villa and hold exhausted post-mortems most evenings before bed. There is no doubt the week is a great success, and yet we had no idea that entertaining a small group of adults every waking minute would be quite so demanding.

While we are preparing our final dinner in the Saturday-morning class, the owner of the villa unexpectedly visits us. He is a lawyer based in Rome who spends occasional weekends at the villa; we are delighted, confused and excited to meet him and thrown into complete disarray when he suggests that we bring all our prepared dishes up to the main house that evening to join him and his wife and several other guests for dinner. One of the older women in our group wonders, when he departs, if there is time for a quick facelift.

That evening the lawyer seats me beside him at the top of the long table and we dine under chandeliers in a room straight from the Middle Ages, complete with busts of emperors above marble fireplaces and vast canvases of battles on the faded walls. I feel exhaustion and privilege in equally deep measures.

Coming back for another season at La Cantinetta was always going to depend on Gianfranco; each time I write letters home, I have a different plan. Towards the very end, some small falling-out triggers the ultimate decision, as if I am just looking for a reason not to come back and face the loneliness and the long, tough hours all over again. I think that I may return at some time, when I have recovered. But my main desire now is to carry back with me all the events, the recipes, the people and the emotions, and calmly spread them out on the floor to begin to make sense of them all. When Valerie, Douglas and I have driven our little group back to Florence airport at the end of the week, we then head on to Perugia so that I can spend my last days in the always-soothing company of Raimondo and Annamaria. This has become the way that I leave Italy.

Baccalà, fegato e ova – più si coce e più s'assoda
Salt cod, liver and eggs – the more you cook them the tougher they become

Back in Sydney, I move straight into a convenient spare bedroom in William's Woollahra flat. But sharing my friend William's small stylish flat is never going to work in the long term. Best friends at first, we become the worst enemies as I struggle naively to make a living by teaching cooking classes at creative venues and William gives up trying not to be gay. We are both deeply unhappy; after one screaming match, we stop talking to each other and I move out.

I teach Italian cooking classes in art galleries, pub kitchens and private homes. In between, there are private catering and short-lived jobs in dubious cafés. Most of all I harbour a sick sense that nothing is working out. I imagined that by my early forties I would be neatly married with three children – and now I don't even have a boyfriend. Acutely lonely, I make the social rounds of dinner parties, restaurants and meeting people for drinks, most of it adding up to emptiness and pointlessness. I launch into an unwise affair with an old friend who has been with the same partner for years; it is as unsatisfactory as all such flings are, because, of course, he doesn't leave her for me. On the one hand, there are more acquaintances with whom to socialise expensively and excessively than I want, and on the other an obsession with the gym and self-control.

The sun in my eyes one Friday evening prevents me from seeing the semi-trailer parked by the side of a busy road and I slide smoothly into it; had there been a passenger beside me he would have perished. Living inner city, I decide thereafter to rely on public transport. A job at a deli crops up, and I accept it with relief – running my own business had been a mistake – only to spend the ensuing months, however, becoming steadily more miserable as the boss chips away at my naturally precarious self-esteem until there is little left. It is almost a relief to be fired, although it means the ignominy of unemployment benefits (at my age – with my talents, skills and education!) and the round of job-hunting. And wondering why I am amounting to nothing, in spite of Italy.

Book Three

1996
Spedaluzzo, near Florence

Chi trova un amico, trova un tesoro
He who finds a friend finds a treasure

Donatella is the one blamed with sending Ignazio, in his new, sleek, silver car, into the wall. I am to hear the Donatella story later on – thanks largely to Alvaro's great affection for gossip. At a great speed, and with blithe disregard for both seatbelts and prior intake of alcohol, he has managed to smash not only the car but also a large proportion of the bones from his right shoulder down to his wrist.

Gianfranco assures me over the phone, eighteen months after we last spoke, that the car's condition is terminal, whereas – *'Grazie a Dio!'* – Ignazio's is not. He is, however, a one-armed member of the operation for now, requiring intensive physiotherapy and not being of much use to La Cantinetta, which is why I am being asked to step into the breach, as it were. And is also why I am, yet again, boarding the train from Rome to Florence dazed with jet lag after the endless flight.

An incident with knives at Fiumicino airport indirectly led to the loss of the bulky fur-lined jacket I arrived in and gratefully shed in the heat of a late European summer. My favourite chef's knife and paring knife were forced by law to travel separately from the rest of my luggage, sealed firmly inside a plastic bag and accompanied by several stern documents that I had laboriously filled out at Sydney airport. There is a collection area at Fiumicino where dubious objects like knives are to be claimed, but after several visits, enquiring of several officials, my knives never materialise. I am back in my beloved Italy, though, and while it is disappointing, the loss of the knives seems entirely unsurprising. (Months later I ask Gianfranco to help me to construct a careful letter to the airport describing my experience. The fact that the letter is never answered also comes as no surprise.) I do feel sad about my jacket, which in my dazed state I presumably left on the train. However, I comfort myself with the prospect of being obliged, towards the end of my stay here, to buy a new one.

Meanwhile, the train is sliding me through hot lime and gold August countryside, the gentle curves of the hills, a sudden river crossing, car factories, a silver gas tanker moving through an avenue of green. We rush through the brief coolness of tunnels; some are so long you forget it is daytime, and then you burst into green and sunshine, your ears popping. Half-broken houses of stone, ruins taken over by ivy perched on hilltops, white roads twisting out of sight, calves lying hotly in fields beside their gently grazing mothers. Gallese, Settebagni, Orte – the towns swish past. Bassano, Attigliano…

I am only to be in Tuscany for a few months, just to help out over the end of a very busy summer; that factor, coupled with the sheer familiarity of my expectations, enables me to barely consider the negative aspects of two years ago. All it takes, then, is the sight of Gianfranco pouchy-eyed and rumpled hair waiting for me at Florence railway station, his face splitting into joy when he sees me, to make it all feel like coming home.

Yet, so many things are different. There is Tonino, for a start, a sturdy toddler with Cinzia's dark beauty and – in evidence already – Gianfranco's personality. There is also Vito, a sixty-something dishwasher whose cheery grandfatherly features both reassure me and remind me (obscurely) of someone from my past. He is leaning in front of the television positioned on the kitchen counter when we arrive, watching the Palio, the annual Siena horse race, with rapt concentration. The kitchen itself is different: now the stoves form an island in the centre of the room so that there are two distinct working areas.

I fling myself into Alvaro's arms, delighted that the old kitchen hand is still there. Gianfranco told me on the journey home that when I left, two years earlier, he trained Alvaro to take my place. Now that I am back, Alvaro will take Gianfranco's position as head chef and I am able to resume my usual role as assistant. Ignazio, thinner and paler, has one arm in an elaborate sling. Ever since the accident, he has been living back at his parents' apartment in Scandicci, enabling me to occupy his large bedroom for the duration of my stay. This bedroom has nearly the same outlook as my previous one had, the green-shuttered windows opening out onto the main road of Via Chiantigiana, the white road disappearing behind ornate wrought-iron railings opposite. The first thing I do is to fling open the windows, then the shutters, and drink in the view and the sounds and the smells, and let the landscape part gently to readmit me.

Ne ammazza più la gola che la spada
Gluttony kills more than the sword does

It is the weekend, and I am already being persuaded to accompany Gianfranco, Cinzia and Tonino to the Isle of Giglio the following Tuesday. Barely unpacked, I prepare a small overnight bag of mainly swimming attire; we will only be gone for two nights. Setting off after service on the Monday night brings back, with a rush of affection, all those times years ago when Gianfranco and I would drive to his village. The drive itself feels similar, late at night and alcohol-fuelled, with the car's headlights carving tunnels out of the blackness and the glowing tips of Gianfranco's cigarette – the only major difference being my position in the back seat and Cinzia's tanned arms enfolding a sleeping child in the front. We arrive at the port at four o'clock in the morning and have several hours to sleep uncomfortably before the ferry departs. I sleep fitfully, briefly, and quietly let myself out of the car just as the sun begins to rise to wander through foreign deserted streets in pursuit of a toilet, in a daze composed of lingering jet lag, tiredness and a seedy hangover.

By the time the ferry arrives, the sun is already scorching rooftops and searing my pallid winter skin. Gianfranco brings coffee and pastries to wake us up properly before driving the car on board. I feel as if I could sleep for a week, but remind myself stoically that the little island escapade will be a perfect pause before launching into three months of hot stoves and long, exhausting hours. Silvio and Carla, Cinzia's parents – at whose holiday house we are staying – are there to meet us and escort us home. They have been on the island all summer and their limbs are the colour of chocolate.

That first day is a series of pleasures. Silvio and Carla take us out on a boat, where we drift for several hours in turquoise water, periodically splashing overboard to seek relief from a blazing sun. Carla fascinates me; covertly I observe the mesmerising way she rubs oil on a perfectly toned body barely reined in by the briefest bikini, her long scarlet fingernails turning pages of a magazine. She frequently applies lipstick with the aid of a tiny mirror. I know from Cinzia that Carla and Silvio met at ballroom dancing classes twenty-odd years ago, and that she has continued the twice-weekly lessons ever since. I am impressed by her glamour, but uneasy about such an excess of vanity. Her neck stretches swan-like out of the water as she doggy-paddles in neat circles around the boat, her fashionable hairdo intact, while the rest of us bomb noisily and swim heartily. Much later, under a canopy of bougainvillaea, we sit down to endless courses of food in the company of Cinzia's brothers and various family friends, who have brought contributions of wine and pastries, cheeses and fruit. We eat and drink long into the night.

Something I eat at the fabulous feast that night manages to ruin the following half-day we have on this island before heading back. The abdominal cramps can only be dealt with by sitting in shallow water at the beach and making regular dashes to the public toilets. All around me holidaymakers robustly hurl themselves into the day. I listen to most of the life story of one of the women who dined with us the previous evening, and then it is time for us to leave, to catch the ferry to the mainland and head back to La Cantinetta. I am apprehensive about my delicacy on the ferry, but in fact halfway through the journey I become extremely hungry. By the time we are back on land, I am almost euphoric with health.

I am astonished at Alvaro's transformation of my old room. His double bed occupies three-quarters of the space, and the rest is a clutter of table and chairs, stereo system complete with enormous loudspeakers, television set, pile upon pile of magazines, a wobbly bookshelf stuffed with more eclectic reading matter, huge ugly ashtrays filled with cigarette butts, a gnawed teddy bear in a soccer jersey, flasks of wine. Clothes, both clean and dirty, drape over every available surface. It exudes cosiness and indolence, unlike the austere bedroom I have moved into, where quivering cobwebs drape from the high ceiling. Every time Gianfranco and Cinzia drive away late at night, it feels as if we are children left alone by unsuspecting parents, to run riot if we choose.

Gianfranco's menu has additions to, and subtractions from, the one two years ago, though some dishes, clearly those that have become his signature ones, are still there. Although I have arrived in the second half of summer, there is still the plethora of gorgeous summer produce dictating the food we make. Furthermore, Gianfranco's funny little garden out the back has now developed into a glorious source of herbs, fruits and vegetables, which we plunder with regularity. There are too many figs, and many lie scattered and skin-split at the base of their trees. They are perfect mashed onto roasted bread.

It is such a pleasurable process carrying with care the tiny zucchini or perfectly ripe tomatoes from the garden into the kitchen and transforming them into a dish, and imbued with a meaning greater than the sum of the small gestures involved. I love most the bay leaves that I snap from their tree, their almost medicinal aroma and especially the note they add to

Crostini con finocchiona e fichi
(Little toasts with fennel salami and figs)

Slice a breadstick thinly and bake slices until crisp. Mash fresh figs in a bowl and season with salt and pepper. Spoon a small amount on to each crostino *and drape elegantly with paper-thin slices of* finocchiona, *fragrant with fennel.*

the *salsa di guanciale*, which I make every few days. This is a spectacular pasta sauce made of ripe plum tomatoes and quantities of *guanciale* – the bacon-like flesh taken from the cheek of a pig with a fat ratio equal to that of the meat. The *guanciale* is sliced into batons five millimetres thick, and added to lots of thinly cut red onions in a large pan, where the flavours intermingle and they turn translucent. Dried chilli is crumbled in at this stage, then a generous slosh of white wine, and finally the tomatoes, which are cut into *spicchi* or thin wedges. And then, the bay leaf! The sauce is brought to a boil, then reduced to a simmer, and after forty minutes it acquires a consistency both jammy and unctuous. It is sublime tossed through spaghetti.

Upstairs, in the space separating Vito the dishwasher's tiny bedroom from Ignazio's larger one, Gianfranco has created a chaotic storeroom to house box after box of wine and mineral water, but also culinary provisions and general junk. I search through squashed cartons until I triumphantly retrieve my set of spring-form baking pans and fluted tart tins. I come across other treasures, like boxes of Tortagel (to glaze cheesecakes and fruit flans) and sachets of vanilla-scented baking powder. There are also endless tins of prunes, purchased by Gianfranco well before my time, to turn into desserts for which he lost inspiration and which, two years previously, I had gradually been using up in moist chocolate cakes that I christened Wombat Cakes. Gianfranco tells me that, for several months after my last departure, customers would drive from Florence to La Cantinetta for a slice of my cheesecake, only to meet with disappointment. Fired with self-confidence, I launch into my *dolce* and, as usual, I am met with an ambivalent attitude from Gianfranco, whose tolerance of my sweet-making is determined utterly by his mood.

The task of washing up my chocolate-coated basins and saucepans, my flour-encrusted chopping boards and rolling pin, my batter-sticky bowls and whisks, starts as a source of amusement for Vito. Those first weeks I am still a novelty. I have no idea what drama is ahead. Meanwhile, I have decided to enrol in a Cordon Bleu course in pastry-making, held conveniently each Tuesday evening over eight weeks in Florence where, as before, I am generally to be found on my day off.

L'appetito vien mangiando!
Appetite comes while you are eating!

Ignazio props his torso on a bench-top and swings the arm which is not in a sling from side to side, looking so like an elephant swinging its trunk that I burst into laughter every time. He smiles wanly – since his accident, he seems permanently wan and somehow diminished – but we are getting along well enough. His father drives him to and from the restaurant, and it is clear that he resents the loss of independence. I have yet to meet his girlfriend, the famous Donatella, of whom everyone speaks in tones of both awe and amusement, and who apparently also does a lot of the ferrying around of Ignazio.

Gossip gleaned from Alvaro and Cinzia reveals that several years previously Donatella and Ignazio were involved,

Lemon cheesecake

Crust
1 packet (250 g) digestive or wheaten biscuits
85 g butter, melted
3 dessertspoons caster sugar

Process the biscuits to fine crumbs and combine
with melted butter and sugar. Press into greased
spring-form pan and chill while making filling.
Preheat oven to 150°C (300°F, Gas mark 2).

Filling
170 g (3/4 cup) caster sugar
600 g cream cheese
Dash vanilla essence
Grated rind 1 lemon
3 eggs

Work the sugar into the cream cheese until well amalgamated.
Add vanilla and lemon rind, then the eggs, one at a time,
beating well after each addition. Pour into chilled crust,
then bake for about an hour or until firm and set.

turbulently, then broke up, only to resume the relationship earlier this year. No one seems to actually approve of Donatella or her effect on Ignazio. Surprisingly, it is Gianfranco who has the few positive things to say about her. (When I meet her, I understand immediately; they are of the same mould.) It was after one of their high-spirited arguments that Ignazio tore off into the night and crashed his car. Somehow one-armed Ignazio manages most of his front-of-house duties, although they are more about public relations. Gianfranco, freed from the kitchen, breezes from table to table being his glorious exuberant self.

Alvaro and I have taken very little time to settle into our positions. In the mornings, with Vito stacking the dishwasher quietly in his corner, I am conscious of the absence of tension as just the two of us work our way through preparation and cooking. Tension is always around Gianfranco, whatever his mood. Alvaro is even and jolly; he whistles and sings along to the radio and comes up behind me to place his hands on my waist.

It is August, and I march past bunches of tiny black grapes lining one side of Via Chiantigiana and, on the other, very small olives that are still green. On those first morning walks, I deliver myself brief, stern lectures about how this time I will behave beautifully, exclude myself less, involve myself more, not cave in to self-imposed, self-absorbed loneliness and gloomy, furtive binge-eating. I am only here for twelve weeks and this time around it feels infinitely more comfortable and familiar.

I return invigorated and sweaty, and shower in the nasty bathroom, Vito and Alvaro still asleep. First into the kitchen (like last time), I perform the ritual of setting up: the enormous pot – or *bagna* – filled with water, salted and straddled across a low flame of gas, the ovens lit, the radio and espresso machine switched on, my list of things to do consulted. Wet-haired Alvaro whistles his way in, secures the apron strings below his paunch, and organises a cigarette and shot of strong coffee.

Gianfranco's four-wheel drive clatters across gravel to a halt mid-morning and the texture of the air changes immediately. Even though he is not in the kitchen with us, his moods continue to be the barometer by which the rest of the day is measured. He is unloading box after box of fruit, vegetables and meat from the markets where he shops daily, and the kitchen is cluttered and chaotic until we have unpacked and dispatched the produce. Cinzia floats and wafts: motherhood has brought out a silliness in her that I had not noticed before, or perhaps it has become her defence at being barked at by Gianfranco.

'*Cazzo fai?*' he is now demanding of me, hovering over my cake-making preparations, and I am babbling like a child as I explain that it is a new and delicious cake, when we both know I should be starting with the pasta sauces, the *cinghiale* (wild boar) or the *anatra* (duck) or the *pappa ai porcini*. Like so many of the ingredients with which we cook and that are not picked up from the markets by Gianfranco, the porcini are delivered to us. This year the *funghaio* (mushroom man) is a comic-faced Florentine called Mario with an enormous moustache and devoid, gratifyingly, of the sleaziness which characterised dear Angelo from two years ago.

Crate upon crate of huge fleshy mushrooms are unloaded from his truck and stacked in the coolroom. The *pappa ai porcini* is a variation on the Tuscan classic *pappa al pomodoro*, that gorgeous sweet tomato soup rendered thick by coarse bread, which simmers until it collapses into a pulp. In the place of tomatoes, the porcini are sliced thickly and left to bubble and perfume the bready broth.

Our next-door neighbour Elio supplies our house wine, the *vino da tavola*. Elio often stands in the kitchen talking to us as we weave around him. Now he is telling us how badly one eats in Genova, where he has just made a short trip – the only good thing was, at least, the pesto. I have been reading in *La Nazione* that, due to a relatively cool summer and the recent spates of rain and thunderstorms, there has been talk of adding sugar during the wine-making process to augment the level of alcohol. I am told this is something Italy has resisted doing until now and I discuss this with Elio, who assures me that in spite of everything he is expecting his wine to be good this year.

Another morning, Ignazio's gentle father arrives clutching a cane basket lined with bright-green vine leaves that contains three types of grape. Apart from the fat green and small black, there is a small white grape called *uva fragola*, so called because of its strawberry flavour. It is intense, perfumed and spicy. I find the flavours of everything to be so sharp, as if the food I eat in Australia is muted, a little bland. The tomatoes, of course, are sweet beyond belief and I eat vast quantities of them, slicked with green oil, accompanying springy, milky mozzarella and bread.

Everything as it should be. And, in spite of the morning lectures, of course I am eating too much again.

I finally meet the famous Donatella, fascinated to see what sort of tempestuous, irresistible woman my sweet angel has moved on to in his romantic life. Suddenly there she is, one damp grey morning, tall and dark with a wiry wildness about her, an easy, loping self-assurance as she ranges restlessly, familiarly, around our kitchen. I see how quickly possessive I become, and instinctively armed to dislike her.

She barely glances my way anyway, even when introduced, and breaks into peals of unexpected, unexplained laughter as Alvaro and I exchange looks. For all his gossipy confidences about her over the weeks, I see that he, too, is prey to some crazed sort of charm she possesses; he is agreeing to go on a snail-gathering expedition with her. They organise buckets and raincoats and the kitchen is suddenly neat and calm without them.

Donatella: the on-again, off-again relationship, perplexes me. I find myself hunting for clues in Ignazio's bedroom about the sort of man he has become. Underneath the bed, drawers reveal little of interest: comic books and magazines, empty cigarette packets and wine labels. There are no tied-up bundles of letters from me and no other evidence that I ever existed for him. Why should there be, after twelve years? And yet I am conscious of obscure disappointment. For all their obvious fondness for me, I have learned how strangely unsentimental both Gianfranco and Ignazio are – their relationship towards me is brotherly, a little dry. It is as if once our affairs of the heart ceased there was no residue of the former passion, nor any great sense that we had made an impact on each other's lives. I wonder if I merely imagine this or if it is I, the strange one, who goes on loving ex-lovers beyond the affair, and can never properly be around them without mentally flickering, periodically, back to images of how great we once were together. I have no desire for either – although there persists something about Ignazio, the shards of remaining sexual tensions, perhaps, which makes me care about other women in his life, and be bothered by them.

Alvaro is cooking the snails that Donatella and he have gathered. First, he laboriously washes them, and then tips them into a pot of cold water. This he places on a low heat to bring to the boil. The snails, at first, are climbing out of the water and up the sides of the pot, but by the time I have rushed upstairs for my camera they have begun to flail and flounder feebly in water too hot for survival, water which is slowly and mercilessly killing them. Of course, as Alvaro points out, it is no crueller than killing lobsters, but my heart has gone out to all those brave little fleshy palpitating bodies struggling from their carapaces up the sides of the pot, only to flop back down again.

The surface of the water is now milky foamy scum, the shells suspended like seashells left by a receding tide, shiny and devoid of their life force. When they have been boiled, they are rinsed and boiled again – the water must be perfectly clear before being added to a separate pot of *odori*: Alvaro's finely chopped celery, carrots, garlic, onion, chilli and wild fennel, which he has softened in olive oil, then with its liquid brought to a simmer before toppling in the snails. He splashes in white wine and, when it has evaporated, adds peeled tomatoes, then leaves the lot to simmer for about half an hour. Over at my chopping board the gentle rattling of shells against the sides of the pot makes me want to cry.

Business is established and steady. Periodically there are functions, which may mean working up to twelve hours with barely a break. Two weddings on one day mean a formal lunch followed by a *merenda* – afternoon tea – for forty people, and when the chaos from that is cleared away we must then set up for the standard evening's à la carte. At least the functions, being immaculately organised, are easy: group food is infinitely less trouble than individual service, with everything arranged and then sent out on platters, the edges wiped briskly clean. Alvaro and I work well together and I find his immeasurable patience, good humour and even temper refreshingly different from the unpredictability and tyranny of Gianfranco.

Occasionally, however, we have the great man back in the kitchen with us. He has been to the markets and brought back a box of artichokes, which Vito is now cleaning, peeling away the outer leaves, cutting sharply across the tops and trimming the bases: artichoke risotto, Gianfranco calls out to Cinzia, is to be one of the daily specials. When he is in the kitchen, I feel as if Alvaro and I unconsciously shrink into the smallness of the space so that no damage can be done and no blame laid. There is Gianfranco at his most magnificent, sloshing olive oil into a wide pan, chopping quickly through the artichokes so they emerge like wafer-thin petals, all his movements firm and economical. In a good mood he instructs us, invites us to dip our fingers into the simmering substance, leaves it on a low heat at a safe stage and disappears, his workstation spotless.

There is an old wood-fired oven out the back, behind the lower function area. I am still a little awed every time I escape the kitchen and step into the beautiful outside world with its two levels of dining, the statuary, the vision of the vineyards beyond the stone walls. Today we are roasting a whole piglet in the oven. Yesterday evening it was stuffed with *frattaglie* (the liver and intestines) tossed with garlic and rosemary, and then stitched neatly up. Bunches of sticks from the vines and cypress branches were fed into the oven to get it going and the fire has now been burning for hours. Vito explains to me how you know when a wood-fired oven is sufficiently hot: the entrance turns white, a condition called *a pane*. The little pig is turning a glorious golden brown and looks as if it is sleeping.

Later in the kitchen, we hear a news report on the radio about someone who has died from eating tiramisu – a particular brand of mascarpone was apparently the culprit. 'I won't be eating it again,' says Vito, who is biting into his snack of a prosciutto-filled panino, warm from the oven, with a glass of Chianti.

Several days later, two policemen appear asking to check our mascarpone – fortunately, the brand we carry is not the one they are looking for, so they are shortly on their way. I continue to serenely whip up batches of the luscious

Risotto ai carciofi
(Artichoke risotto)

*Prepare two saucepans, one containing about
1 litre of simmering chicken stock and the
other containing a little olive oil.
Prepare 8 medium-sized artichokes by removing the
tough outer leaves and trimming their bases to about 2
cm. Cut across top leaves, halve, then quarter. Leave in a
bowl of water with a lemon wedge until ready to use.
Finely chop together 1 medium onion and 2 fat garlic
cloves and soften them in heated olive oil. Drain artichoke
quarters and add to pan, seasoning to taste, and sauté for
several minutes. Toss in 1 1/2 cups Arborio rice and, stirring
continuously, allow to be coated with oil and vegetables for
about 5 minutes. Ladle in several cups (or to cover) of stock,
lower heat and, stirring frequently, simmer rice. When it has
absorbed most of the stock, add another cup and continue
this until the rice is nearly cooked – al dente (chewy) –
which may take 25 to 30 minutes. Remove from heat, add
a knob of butter, a handful of freshly grated Parmesan
and finely chopped parsley. Cover the pan and leave for 5
minutes, check seasoning and then serve immediately.*

cream, which I flavour with grated orange rind and layer in individual glass cups with coffee-dunked biscuits and cocoa.

Meglio un giorno da leone che cento da pecora
Better one day as a lion than a hundred as a sheep

Vito initially reminds me of Annunzio from Robespierre, the restaurant where I worked on the Isle of Elba, but then I begin to see how little alike they really are. Vito's cosy grandfatherly quality reveals itself, I come to perceive, as a bitter provincial pettiness. He gossips nastily about the people in his life who have let him down, and lacks any genuine sympathetic interest in the lives of others. Annunzio, for all his history of failures, disappointments and wrong choices, had still offered the solidity of his patient listening, his homespun wisdom and advice, whereas there is an insistent whine threading through everything Vito says and a shiftiness in his eyes, which rarely hold your own for very long.

But for now our friendship flowers in the inevitable way that close working relationships do; more often than not it is, after all, just the three of us in the kitchen, Vito, Alvaro and la Veeky, muddling along easily enough together and often sharing meals, linked by the common bond of being staff versus principals. The cubby hole which was once Vera's, and is now Vito's, bedroom is even more spartan –

the narrow bed neatly made up with an extra blanket folded at its foot seems all the private space he possesses, stark and impersonal as a motel room. He rarely speaks about another life, a past, a youth, a family; phone calls and visitors and groups of noisy animated diners never come for him. He darkly addresses the sink of frying pans and pots with a vigorous scrubbing in which violence seems grudgingly suppressed. Within weeks, all my chocolate-lacquered, dough-encrusted equipment has ceased to amuse him and, now betrayed by heavy sighing, merely exasperates.

È più forte di me
It is stronger than me

Early September and the weather is cooling down. My morning walks take me past grapes that bulge in thick fat bunches of burgundy through the endlessly unscrolling vineyards. It is the season of *schiacciata all' uva* – the sweet flatbread studded with new grapes – and in all the Florentine bakeries large slabs of moist sticky bread dough, glittering with black-crimson grapes, are sold by the hundred grams or by the square. I make up batches from the vast quantities of grapes plundered by Alvaro from neighbouring vineyards after his vinous lunches.

I am determined to get them perfectly right – although my dough is inevitably too thick and puffy, when thin is best. They are always delicious, but always generate heated discussion around the table of tasters: too much like bread, not light enough, too sweet, not enough grapes, too many grapes. One time, bored with the *uva* component, I decide to add sultanas, walnuts, pine nuts, orange rind and coarsely chopped cooking chocolate to the mixture, which I then shape into a careful plait and brush with egg yolk. It looks sensational when baked, though we all agree it is a little heavy.

The olives, meanwhile, are still green. Our old friend Vincenzo Sabatini, with whom I went to stay when Gianfranco and I broke up, towers above everyone in our kitchen. He explains how this is the optimum stage for turning them into oil so that it emerges a little tart, and fruity, glorious green. Only in Tuscany and Umbria, he goes on, are the olives not left to fall to the ground (where they bruise and spoil and attract worms) but are still picked from the trees – by hand, occasionally, though now mostly by machines.

Vincenzo's visits are always highlights: he and his wife Claudia were always like second parents to me, and it still feels that way. Mid-mornings, the kitchen will suddenly seem diminished with the arrival of Vincenzo, his huge bulk encased in denim overalls, who helps himself to a panino of prosciutto and tips an entire glass of white wine down his throat in a single gulp as he stands there telling us stories. One day he draws me aside to give me some advice. Never, he warns, give away a complete recipe; always remember to leave out just one ingredient. I wrap my arms around the familiarity of his girth, cosily complicit.

Gianfranco is making a little pizza with dough left over from the previous evening's *schiacciata all' uva*. There

Schiacciata all' uva
(Sweet flatbread with grapes)

20 g fresh yeast
100 g sugar
800 g strong bread flour
125 ml water
Olive oil
1 kg small black grapes

Dissolve the yeast in lukewarm water together with 1 tablespoonful of sugar and another of flour. Allow to rise for an hour. Add all the flour, 2 more tablespoons of sugar, plus 3 of olive oil, and work well – the dough should be soft and elastic. Prove for another hour, then press into an oiled baking tin; the dough should be double the size of the tin and drape over the sides. Scatter over half the washed and dried grapes, a little sugar and some oil. Fold over the rest of the dough and scatter on the remaining grapes, sugar and oil. Bake in a preheated 180°C (350°F, Gas mark 4) oven for about an hour.

have been fewer customers these past evenings and they are leaving earlier. This is an excuse for Gianfranco to do the cooking he rarely does any more. He is stretching the dough out into the thinnest possible disc and scattering it with olive oil, salt and needles of fresh rosemary. He slides it into a very hot oven for five minutes, and when he removes it we fall upon it, gobbling it down hot and crunchy with transparent slices of prosciutto, our chins shiny with oil.

Another morning he attempts a *sfogliata di rape*, trying to remember how his mother used to make it. I had almost forgotten the snake-shaped pastries he and I used to eat cold in the early morning kitchen at his village, washed down with red wine, but now watching him the vision returns with force. The *rape* (turnip tops), he has cooked the previous day, large bunches of deep green leaves similar to spinach which he simmers in oil, garlic and a little *brodo* – broth. The result is salty beyond belief. (*'Serpentato!'* exclaims Gianfranco, furious the rare times his cooking goes wrong.)

Now he is finely chopping the vegetable and stirring through freshly grated Parmesan and a few sloshes of olive oil. The dough is wafer-thin and fragile; he rolls it out and fills it with the *rape* mixture, curling it up into sausages, then coiling them into a baking dish. When they are extracted, all golden and crunchy, we sample them. He admits to not being completely happy: the dough should have been even thinner, almost completely transparent so the vegetable shows through. Silverbeet, he is telling us, is what Mamma always used – and I look over at him and see that this is one of the ways I love him best, his cheeks curving into the smile of pride which mentions of his mother unfailingly inspire.

His *sfogliata* I find delicious, probably more refined than I remember hers being.

Ho una fame da lupo
I have the hunger of a wolf

We rarely eat together after service, the principals continuing to make their escape as early as they can. I have my private doubts about the little family of Gianfranco, Cinzia and Tonino, but I can see that they are trying hard, or at least Gianfranco is now trying hard, while Cinzia always has. Ignazio is still at his parents' apartment with his broken healing limb, visiting a physiotherapist, still dogged by the black-eyed, wild, laughing Donatella in a relationship that continues to baffle me. She seems in such contrast to me. I wonder what common qualities we could possibly possess, and meanwhile reciprocate the disdain she constantly spears in my direction. I also wonder if she knows the history of Ignazio and me.

As long as it is still mild enough for outdoor dining, a motley group of us collects around a table with our assorted meals, but once the evening cold begins in earnest, Alvaro and I fall into the cosiness of meals in his room. Like a middle-aged couple, we settle in front of television on the unmade bed, plates in our laps, chatting desultorily, drinking too much. Alvaro stubs out cigarettes into malodorous, unemptied ashtrays. His socks kicked free of the clogs he wears for work give off a warmly vegetal, faintly fetid odour; we push aside clothing and newspapers to make room for the civilisation of dinner, and there is a quality of such homeliness, safety and companionship in the room that I begin to look forward to the evenings. His girlfriend waitresses in a restaurant several villages away and occasionally after work will drive over to visit. I like Rita, who is birdlike with thick-lensed glasses and a sort of bossy maternal way with Alvaro. Like so many couples, this one strikes me as odd.

I am quite enjoying my pastry-making course at the Cordon Bleu Institute. The classes take place in a building near Via Ghibellina and the apartment Ignazio and I used to share. Up a flight of steps I carry my bags of Florentine shopping each Tuesday and settle at one of the chairs arranged in a circle in the big kitchen.

Annamaria and Silvia are surely too slender and too beautiful to be pastry chefs – they look like models, young women in their twenties whose aprons and tailored trousers seem too smart for the business of food preparation. Their long bony fingers with pearly manicured nails move with deft confidence, however, through each procedure, and their final creations invariably provoke sighs of admiration.

Each week the making of several different desserts and pastries is taught, demonstrated, then tasted; the class is encouraged to participate after the demonstrations. And so we whisk egg whites endlessly in copper bowls, simmer diced apple in butter and spices before filling apple charlottes, gently heat sugar syrups, and roll out pastry. Whenever pastry is concerned, it is Silvia who takes over. *'Ha le mani fredde'* – she has cold hands – explains Annamaria, essential

Zabaglione

8 large egg yolks
100 g caster sugar
250 ml dry Marsala

*In a large, heatproof bowl, beat the egg yolks and sugar
with a whisk until they are thick and pale, then beat in the
Marsala. Set the bowl over a saucepan of barely simmering
water and keep beating until the mixture becomes a thick
foam – electric beaters make this less labour-intensive!
Serve accompanied by* savoiardi *biscuits for dunking.*

for the delicate matter of pastry-making and the difference between light and leaden.

There are twelve students, mostly Italian and mostly women, but there are a few Asians, a South American, a German and me. Over six weeks, we bond little more than the exchange of shy smiles during some procedure. At the end of the evening, when we are urged to stay, chat and sample the cooking, I am too impatient to be away, striding briskly towards the looming back of the Duomo through the darkening streets to reach my bus in time for the return home. I am also aware, halfway into the expensive course, that I am not learning as much as I had hoped – that, in fact, I know more than I thought I did.

Un buon vino, un buon uomo e
una bella donna durano poco
A good wine, a good man and a
pretty woman last a short time

At La Cantinetta I have slipped so effortlessly into the role of dessert-and-cake-maker – it is my greatest joy. I continue to bake my famous cheesecakes in a wealth of variations. I bake almost-flourless chocolate truffle cakes lacquered with dark icing, and enormous carrot cakes studded with walnuts and smothered in cream cheese icing. I simmer oranges until they are soft enough to whizz to a paste, then fold through ground almonds and sugar and eggs and transform it into Claudia Roden's Middle Eastern orange cake.

Chocolate truffle cake

100 g dark chocolate, chopped coarsely
100 g unsalted butter, cut into 8 pieces
3 large eggs
150 g caster sugar
50 g plain flour

Preheat oven to 200°C (400°F, Gas mark 6). Melt chocolate and butter in double boiler and set aside to cool a little. Beat eggs with sugar till pale and thick, then stir through chocolate mixture – or use a whisk (it's easier). Add sifted flour and beat well for 3 minutes with electric mixer. Pour into buttered cake pan and cook for about 20 minutes. Cool for 5 minutes in pan before turning out. When cold, ice with the glaze.

Glaze
80 g dark chocolate
10 g unsalted butter
100 ml thickened cream
Cocoa powder

Melt dark chocolate and unsalted butter. Bring thickened cream to the boil in a separate saucepan and whisk into the chocolate until smooth and shiny. Pour over the cake and sift cocoa powder over the top. Chill before serving.

I make pies and tarts, falling back almost guiltily on my own recipe for perfect pastry, one I have been using since I was about twelve years old, which never lets me down regardless of the temperature of my hands. I mostly make apple pies with lattice lids, which I gild with egg yolk for a gorgeous golden finish.

Often it is a *crostata*, a pastry shell, which I fill with custard and top with fruit. The mixed berry ones always look spectacular with their glazed tumble of blueberries, raspberries, blackberries and other tiny berries whose names I do not even know. Sometimes the egg yolks are so brilliantly yellow that the resulting *crema pasticciera* (custard) emerges lustrous and luscious, and it is such a pleasure to smooth it thickly into the cooled, cooked base of the flan.

Like last time, Gianfranco in a cheerful frame of mind will tease, applaud and indulge me in my sweet-making, but when tense and short-tempered, which is mostly, he will bead his eyes malevolently in my direction and so I gallop to a hasty conclusion, my heart pounding foolishly like a reprimanded child.

For large functions he often sets me the task of creating enormous *crostate* on a special wooden board. This involves quadrupling the amount of pastry I usually make, rolling it out in sections carefully and neatly onto the board, pinching up a border all the way around and filling it with a creamy custard. Gianfranco always insists on helping me with the topping and it is one of those precious moments when we are quietly working together, our heads lowered in focused concentration as we arrange kiwi fruit, strawberries, blueberries and figs in exquisite patterns, joking and teasing, joined in our shared passion for the artistry of food.

Guido, the bearded banker, brings into the kitchen a plate of *ovoli* he found growing by the road. His delicate fingers lift the mushrooms to show me their resemblance to hard-boiled eggs. These are the most valuable of mushrooms, he explains, costing up to 80,000 lire (€40) a kilo, pointing out how the white 'shell' has been partly peeled away to expose a rich golden 'yolk'. Gianfranco has joined us; Guido always cheers him up, loosens the tension around his mouth and eyes and has him laughing, which he is doing now, expertly inserting the point of his tiny knife under the white part of the mushrooms and lifting it off so we can admire the perfect gold fungus beneath. I remember eating these once in Siena with Piero, cooked simply in butter and tossed with shreds of *tagliolini*, very thin fresh pasta.

Tonight we all dine together when the kitchen closes early. Ignazio and Cinzia set one of the inside tables, while Gianfranco is preparing carpaccio of lean, pale-crimson eye fillet, adorning it with slender slices of Guido's *ovoli*, which he has tossed in new green olive oil. I contribute the pungent *pecorino stagionato* I bought earlier in Greve, still encased in its waxy paper, and one of my apple pies. Buried in rice in the fridge I am saving up the precious black truffle presented to me by Mario, our *fungaio*.

Having started this season at La Cantinetta plump, I grimly resolved not to become plumper. I am sliding there in spite of all the promises that I made to myself on the flight coming over, all my earnest diary entries and letters to friends and family. '*È più forte di me*' – I can't help it – is a saying I hear regularly and one which I find I use increasingly as an excuse for second helpings, too much bread, the chunk of tangy Parmesan that I nibble on slow evenings with a glass of Chianti. I glance at Guido's much younger wife, a beautiful woman with skin a peachy flawlessness and the body of a ballerina. She once confided to me that she never diets, but simply avoids consuming both bread and wine. Bread and wine! A sacrifice too great for a woman whose excesses are commonly justified on the grounds of loneliness, failure to be appreciated or cared about, infrequent communication from Australia, and the gibes and criticisms of Gianfranco and Ignazio.

There is an absence of mirrors – La Cantinetta is almost devoid of any, except the small high one in the bathroom, which requires tremulous balancing on the edge of the tub for unsatisfactory viewing. I find this lack of reflection unsettling; as if my own image were the only core of reassuring familiarity I have in this temporary strange world. Guido's wife is the sort of graceful poised Italian woman beside whom I feel large and clumsy, to whom I blurt out my insecure inner life over too much late-night Chianti, conscious of being too eager and too friendly and too, finally, misunderstood. A messy splashing around beside her self-contained creaminess and her slender dignity, only vindicated, at least a little, when Gianfranco carves himself off a thick-crusted wedge of my apple pie and sinks his teeth into it with a look of rapture. At least there are my desserts and cakes to redeem me, to rescue me, to restore my value.

Crostata di mele
(Apple pie)

*Make up a batch of my perfect pastry (see Fruit Tart recipe,
p. 110). Line a greased pie dish with the rolled-out, larger
half of it and trim. Fill with apples you have stewed with a
little sugar and strip of lemon rind. Roll out the other half
of pastry and fit neatly over the apple. Prick all over with
fork and brush with beaten egg yolk. Bake until golden in
a moderately high (180°C, 350°F, Gas mark 4) oven.*

It is autumn and the menu has changed again. I am plunging my hands – almost up to elbows – in Gianfranco's *salsa di pecora*, the mutton sauce he has been slowly simmering all morning and which we will serve with rigatoni. To the standard base of onion, celery and garlic is added the dismembered sheep he carved up earlier, several bones, some ordinary minced topside, then later the red wine and the peeled tomatoes. I am peeling the flesh from the bones. It is a fatty sauce with a fatty earthy aroma reminding me of the heavenly oxtail sauce, the *salsa di coda*, we were making two years ago.

On the radio, Neneh Cherry sings 'It's a Man's World' and in his little corner Vito thumps the hood of the dishwasher shut. Alvaro is mixing the batter for the popular deep-fried chicken and vegetables, which we serve tumbling out of stiff paper cones: he whisks together eggs and white wine, then one cup of flour and in its still lumpy stage folds through chopped chicken thighs.

Farro, the ancient grain spelt, has become the fashionable item this season, and so we are turning it into soups and salads. There is a pot of steadily simmering, thickening soup of spelt and porcini mushrooms alongside an asparagus sauce to be served with tagliatelle.

Earlier I watched Gianfranco and Alvaro prepare fresh pigs' cheeks to make *guanciale*, the large cheeks placed into a container and covered completely with rock salt. In several days they will be ready for the addition of garlic, herbs and lots of pepper, before being hung for several weeks. Already hanging from the rafters in the

Pollo fritto
(Fried chicken)

1 kg chicken thighs, halved
2 eggs
1/2 cup white wine
230 g (1 cup) plain flour
Sage and rosemary, roughly chopped
Salt
Vegetable oil

Whisk together all ingredients (except chicken), until
smooth. Add chicken and set aside for about an
hour. Deep-fry in very hot vegetable oil till crisp and
golden. Drain on paper towels, and serve in paper
cones sprinkled with sea salt and lemon wedges.

rarely used upstairs television room are *prosciutti* of various sizes. They are treated the same way, though being so much larger they are left under salt for a month. They must hang for a year, the salt 'cooking' them and providing flavour. Vito tells me that *prosciutti* used to be draped over fireplaces, but nowadays they are hung in rooms ventilated by enormous fans to dry them out; in the final phase they are left in damp cool cellars. The drying must happen quickly, or they will start to rot.

Gianfranco's moodiness and volatility keep us steady and alert. I begin to see in my endless meditations, letters home, or when I plunge off on my morning walks, how he is the essential centrifugal force holding the rest of our weaker souls together, and without him we would fall apart. No one else possesses his authority, although I observe how much in his shadow Ignazio has grown up and developed, how earnestly he seeks to imitate and emulate. Sweet little Ignazio, who drinks steadily throughout the day, must fill in the spaces of Gianfranco's gradually increasing absences, but 'the essence' is always there to hold us together.

Although capable of admirable efficiency, Alvaro also drinks day and evening, and slides easily into sloppiness. I persist with my private stern lectures and diary entries, reminding myself this 'season' is a mere matter of months after which I will return to my sane and comfortable Sydney life, my Paddington flat and my trivial, tedious routines. I am here to absorb, learn and be inspired rather than be sucked back into the wells of loneliness and self-contempt.

It is taking me all this time to understand that what I see as his failure to appreciate me and to constantly acknowledge my work is perhaps Gianfranco's professionalism, the detachment necessary to steer his team and ensure its flow; that in reality it may be a measure of my stubbornly low self-esteem – and that what the experience could be teaching me, among realms of other great lessons, is self-reliance; that the reason I should work hard, create magnificent food and always do my best is not a needy search for approval and praise, but because it is a worthy way to live.

Amor nuovo va e viene, amore vecchio si mantiene
New love comes and goes but old love remains

Unfailingly, I am moved by the rare displays of Gianfranco's solicitude. One evening we receive a visit from Emilio, our detergent sales representative, a gingery pink and fleshy man habitually dressed in khaki. He and a boisterous group of friends have been dining and Emilio, drunk, has run into the kitchen and scooped up the bread-and-butter pudding – which I had painstakingly been making as a gift for Ignazio's mother – and disappeared. The car tyres squeal away, laughter floating from the windows as Alvaro and I gape at each other. Gianfranco, of course, is informed immediately: his face whitens with fury and he swears he will have no more dealings with this man, should he dare show his face.

A month later he does. Again, he comes in with a group of friends, who all drink too much, and again he erupts into the kitchen to greet us all. Alvaro and Ignazio are sycophantic and respond to his jokes. I have turned my back in cold contempt, fascinated to see what, if anything, Gianfranco will do.

Gianfranco finishes his telephone conversation and turns to Emilio. He is icy. He says that he wants nothing more to do with him, and that he will be buying our cleaning agents elsewhere, and that, yet again, Emilio has that evening drunkenly created *'un casino'* in the restaurant. But most significantly it was the crime of having taken off with the *dolce*, which la Veeky had spent an entire day slaving over (how I love this man), which means the relationship is over. *'Finito, chiuso!'*

There stands Emilio, smooth-talking and florid, reduced to a puffy ridiculous figure by Gianfranco's speech and quite shocked by it, and I am discreetly watching Gianfranco, who had clearly been upset by the whole incident too, but who possesses such integrity and loyalty that he is barely quivering. I have never seen him more magnificent; he takes my breath away. Emilio seems to melt, and then he is gone.

There are so many things about this restaurant that I love. It seems to be the perfect Chianti experience – its cosy interior with fresh flowers and beautiful glassware on each lunch-laid table; tiny candles in containers and pot plants and intimate corners; the dusty bottles of ancient Chiantis arranged around the walls.

I have fewer Australian visitors this year and remind myself not to do what I did last time; namely, pounce on them and demand to know if they think I look fat. Of course, I am fat again because the circumstances and issues are the same: the dire combination of low self-esteem and working, long gruelling hours, while having constant access to unlimited amounts of irresistibly lovely food and wine. I just have to open the fridge door: a haunch of Parmesan cheese reposes among black figs, huge glorious deep-green leaves of rocket, fat ridged zucchini, tiny golden *finferi* mushrooms, a plethora of such gorgeous food, food I will never find in Australia, food which is provocatively of the season and the place, so freshly of the moment.

I am regrettably more conscious of the times when I am barked at by Gianfranco as if I were some lowly hired help than of the other precious moments when I watch him create amazing dishes or merely singe the hair of a duck over the open flame before hacking it up into small segments. The grace and economy that emerge whenever he cooks I find almost arousing; it is one of the rare times I feel stirring in me something of the old passion he used to evoke.

I am watching as he mixes cheeses: *'Uno sperimento'* – an experiment – he says grandly and mysteriously, as he grates expensive fontina with fresh pecorino and mashes it into Gorgonzola, adding a handful of grated Parmesan. I ask him when he invented this experiment and he explains how, delayed that morning in a queue of cars, he dreamed it up. Now he smears it over cooked polenta and slides it into the oven. When he extracts it, golden and bubbling, he serves it with grilled spicy sausage and pork belly. Of course, it is sensational. I keep flashing back to images of him sitting impatiently in his big four-wheel drive stuck somewhere between Florence and Spedaluzzo, his mind moving on to recipes, food combinations, menu ideas. How can I not love this man?

The figs have come and gone. The huge tree out the back in Gianfranco's garden has yielded such a feast of them, too many for us to gather and use. They are scattered everywhere, skins spilt to reveal their crimson hearts, bird-pecked, rotting. Their dark leaves we use to line the platters for antipasti or for special functions; I have made endless fig *crostate*. On my walks, the landscape is changing, the air crisper now, veils of mist hanging over vineyards and olives finally beginning to turn black. The fields are stripped of the grapes, hand-plucked by the groups of itinerant African pickers.

One morning I contemplate how the countryside consists of so many different perspectives; it is ever-changing, and every bend in the road throws up a whole new vision of gorgeousness, a little like those glass domes of snow you shake, and when the snow settles it is a rearranged beauty. On my walks I ponder what I will be cooking that day and the changes to the menu. I think about making potato gnocchi and the mutton sauce and a salad of spelt and porcini mushrooms with shavings of the black truffles Mario brings us. The porcini will be turned into a silky sauce for tagliatelle. There may be a need for more minestrone, perfumed by the wild thyme called *pepolino*. We are serving *fettunta* with a garlicky mix of chicory and *toscanelli* beans and a final slick of good oil; *ribollita*, minestrone thickened with stale bread,

Fettunta al cavolo nero
(Garlic bread with cavolo nero)

*Strip the leaves from the stalks of a bunch of cavolo nero,
and drop them into boiling salted water until just cooked.
Drain and squeeze out the excess water. Toast slices of rustic
bread, then rub both sides with a clove of garlic. Drizzle
extra virgin olive oil over this, then arrange cavolo nero on
the top, grinding some black pepper over it, and drizzling
with an extra thread of olive oil. Serve while still hot.*

simmers to creamy thickness. The oxtail sauce I most enjoy making is on the list, as is the wild-boar sauce.

The chestnuts are here. Dotted around Florence are the braziers where they are toasted, then served in twisted cones of paper. Vito is telling us his preference when dealing with chestnuts: boil them in their shells with borlotti beans and a little bit of charcoal which, he claims, rids the chestnuts of their acidity. You then suck the flesh out of the shells. For the next month, he is explaining – clattering pots out of the dishwasher, hooking them up over the stoves, where they briefly swing – chestnuts are eaten with everything, and then you suddenly realise how sick of them you are. He talks about how rabbits become fat in this period by scraping the chestnut meat from their shells – which makes me briefly consider how delicious those rabbits might then be to eat.

One afternoon I make a dramatic departure from the kitchen in tears, due a combination of premenstrual tension and a reprimand delivered to Alvaro and me by Ignazio about our performance the previous Sunday lunch. (Gianfranco had been absent, Alvaro had been drunk, I felt that I had worked doubly hard to compensate and Ignazio had upbraided us both, furious, for the fact that we did not give Vito a hand.) I sit on my unmade bed feeling misunderstood and underappreciated and exhausted when there is a knock on my door. It is Vito, with a bowl of chestnuts for me to eat now while they are still hot. Feeling like a child, I eat the whole bowl in the dark, shakily, and cheer up.

BOOK THREE

A chi ha fame è buono ogni pane
All bread is good when you're hungry

At least one afternoon each week, I board the bus for Greve with my bag of laundry. I drift, browsing through postcards on the racks in the arcade, pressing my nose to the glass of Falorni's famous butcher shop, selecting a portion of cheese from the deli, sitting with a beer in the main piazza café. One afternoon Vito asks if he may accompany me. We stroll through the town, across a leaf-swirled stone bridge below which murky water stagnates, licking the *gelati* he has bought for us, not talking much. Then Vito completely astounds me: he asks me if I can give him '*un bacino*' – a little kiss. Memories of Lorenzo in Florence all those years ago come flooding back. I feel briefly frozen, stunned by my failure yet again to interpret human behaviour. Suppressing the shock and revulsion I feel, I laugh his question off, clumsy as a teenager, mumbling words to the effect of valuing our friendship. And, in the same way that my rejection offended Lorenzo, I can see I am wounding stupid old Vito, who seems to withdraw into himself. The companionable quality of the air has shifted, and we return to town and to the bus stop in a silence heavy with reproach. I feel utterly miserable – Vito beside me on the bus with head turned away seems to be throwing out waves of venom through every pore.

From that afternoon onwards, our relationship is for ever changed. In the kitchen, he neither looks at nor talks to me, thus setting the pattern for the remainder of my stay. I tell

Alvaro about the incident and he finds it merely amusing, and yet he is never in the kitchen when, together and alone, Vito and I work in silence, brittle with tension and hostility. I wait for Vito to stab me. I begin to dread being on my own with him, especially when I am obliged to deposit my pile of sweet-making paraphernalia on the sink for him to wash. He begins to snarl and swear and crashes them into the sink, muttering audibly for me to hear about how pissed off he is with the mess I always make with my 'fucking desserts'.

The violence in both his voice and his movements terrifies me. I actually begin to rinse the chocolatey basins, the custard-filmed saucepans and the sticky sides of spring-form pans before taking them over to his territory. It makes no impression on the contempt he spits at me, and I am finally obliged to pour the whole story out to Gianfranco. Unlike Alvaro, he takes it seriously, though I can see how the episode constitutes another source of anxiety for him. I seek hastily to reassure him, when it is really me who so desperately needs that reassurance from him.

I find myself beginning furtively to count the days. The days, turning seriously cool, turning cold, are bringing fewer and fewer customers. Gianfranco prepares for his hunting trip down south in the company of Cinzia's father. Pino, the butcher, will come and give Ignazio a hand – essentially, it will just be the five of us.

Each Wednesday I begin a diet, which lasts until Saturday evening when boredom or exhaustion compels me to cave in to the self-gratification of food. I am plump, or *'in carne'* – meaty – as one of Gianfranco's friends remarked jovially one day, with spectacular insensitivity. Once again I retreat into novels in my little perch up by the stove, while the others slump in front of televised football matches. I had vowed not to exclude myself, but I have no control over the wells of emptiness inside me, the need to be loved, hugged and reassured of my loveliness. Everyone irritates me: Ignazio and his moodiness, stupid giggling Cinzia, inexhaustible Alvaro, the utterly contemptible Vito spitting out his loathing for me in the safety of an empty kitchen. The bantering they go in for reminds me of children, and I long to be in the company of sensible, intelligent, calm adults who discuss interesting things.

There have been visits, though too rarely this time, from dear Piero. One night he takes me to a Pugliese restaurant in Florence specialising in horse-meat dishes, and over fatty salami which nearly makes me gag, I make a brave attempt at describing my life positively. And with him I am able; with him, away from La Cantinetta, I am reminded how much it is all giving me. And that, like last time, the measure of my dissatisfaction there is invariably the measure of my self-worth. I wish I could always see it this clearly.

'Italia sì, Italia no. Una pizza in compagnia. La banda di buco!' sings Alvaro as he swings into the kitchen for evening service. Shortly after lunch he had disappeared, driving his Fiat Bambino down the hill to visit a friend and to 'take two or three glasses'. He is visibly drunk. He sets up his workstation sloppily, pouring himself more wine, fiddling impatiently with the radio dial, pinching the fold of flesh around my waist as he passes behind me. My heart sinks: this has happened before and it means carrying Alvaro through the evening, double-checking every order that comes in, ensuring Ignazio stays well away, praying we have few customers.

From my side of the stoves, I watch him discreetly over my pots of bubbling pasta: so much about the kitchen is anticipating several steps ahead, and I find I am doing this for both of us. Quartering radicchio hearts to be brushed with oil then grilled, thinly slicing bread for *crostini*, dunking battered vegetables into the deep-fryer: these are the little side-jobs we generally share in a harmonious, unspoken system and which I now assume on my own. At the same time I am anxious to keep Alvaro happy, so I humour him as well.

Then Ignazio brings back into the kitchen a plate of eye fillet steak, which he describes as disgusting, a disgrace, inedible – and at this point the blurry drunken amiability turns savage. As Ignazio leaves, Alvaro unhooks the side of beef from the fridge and brings it over to the chopping block, presumably to saw off another steak, but instead, his face contorted, he heaves the entire thing into one of the big bins. Vito and I look on shocked. Ignazio has seen nothing and I am racing over to Alvaro, telling him that everything will be alright and that we can wash the meat and I will cut the required steak, and even do the grilling, if necessary. I have watched both Gianfranco and Alvaro do the mains so often – many of them involve merely reheating; otherwise it is a simple matter of grilling or frying – so I feel confident. Alvaro is insisting he is perfectly fine, and then he is on the floor, his clogs scrabbling to re-establish a grip.

Radicchio al forno
(Roast radicchio)

Cut one radicchio in half (per serving) and place halves in a baking dish or small ramekin. Generously lace each radicchio with extra virgin olive oil, one crushed clove of garlic, salt and pepper. Place in preheated 180°C (350°F, Gas mark 4) oven until sizzling and golden, turn after 5 minutes and season again. Then roast for another 5 to 10 minutes.

This is a scene so farcical that I feel like laughing. If only the customers knew! If only Gianfranco would materialise at that moment! The enormous haunch of beef is still sticking out of the bin, enough Florentine steaks to feed thirty hungry men, and the head chef is in a comical sprawl on the floor, Vito and la Veeky in their mutual hostility unable to seek help from each other. Alvaro scrambles somehow to his feet, and the evening is able to continue, but my heart is pounding.

Amicizie e maccheroni, sono meglio caldi
Friendships and macaroni are best when warm

It just happens. One minute I am forking the last of the chicken salad into my mouth, wiping oil from its corner, stretching along the length of bunched-up sheets and blankets on Alvaro's unmade bed, and the next Alvaro is crawling on top of me, breathing rapidly, his cigarette mouth covering mine. His hands are on my breasts, rippling down my thighs, and his tongue in my ear. I respond, the past month of feeling unloved and meaningless exploding into pleasure and the unfamiliarity of sex. I am not in love with this dear sweet man, yet our arms are fiercely claiming each other, returning me to a sense of my being the womanly, desirable self that I thought had gone: I love him for this. We wriggle around and kiss wetly, and then I manage to slow us both down, slide away, smile with sweet foolishness and button my jeans.

He lights a cigarette and watches me, amused, as I gather up my salad bowl and cutlery and empty wine glass and thank him ironically for having me and pad back to the room I inhabit down the hall. In the kitchen the following morning, I am relieved that it has changed little between us, that in the place of the self-consciousness I was fearing is, on the contrary, a lighter, freer air, and Alvaro's hands on my waist when he walks past me remain a fraction longer than usual.

Gianfranco is showing us the ancient Tuscan method of cooking *toscanelli* beans in an empty Chianti flask. He tips them in and adds water, garlic, salt, sage and a little olive oil, then seals the neck of the flask with cotton wool. The flask is then placed onto a cloth in a deep pot of boiling bubbling water, where it will continue to cook for about three hours. By this stage, he tells us, the beans will have absorbed all the water and be ready to eat. I am already imagining them alongside one of Pino's fat spicy sausages.

Hate and love swirl through the kitchen like waves of shimmering heat. Vito persists with his private war against me – my telling Gianfranco about it has not assisted at all – but in compensation there is Alvaro's wink across the stoves, *'una bella trombatina'* – a great fuck – whispered in my ear, and only several more weeks before it is all over, anyway.

Alvaro and I have succumbed to panting, hungry sex several times, the television turned up loud to prevent sleeping Vito from hearing anything, and I am conscious of

Faglioli lessi
(Boiled beans)

Soak 500 g of dried cannellini beans overnight. The next
day, cook them in their soaking water, together with 1
to 2 sticks chopped celery, 3 to 4 cloves of garlic peeled
and chopped, 1 peeled and chopped onion, 1 roughly
chopped ripe tomato, and salt. When they have come
to the boil, lower heat and simmer until tender. Drain,
check seasoning and drizzle with extra virgin olive oil.
This is lovely as a vegetable accompaniment or
toppled on to grilled, garlic-rubbed bread.

feeling luminous, that near-forgotten sense of being desired and desirable. Plump I may be, but Alvaro wants me. Rita has barely visited in this latter period and I am grateful; tangled up with the luminosity is the treachery of my behaviour. I am aware, as well, that it is not properly love, this feverish coming-together of Alvaro and me, and more a neediness and a loneliness, a companionable exchange of comfort and caress. I smile inanely at unexpected moments.

Even the baptisms and communion lunches are thinning out. Cinzia has been rarely with us, spending most of the time at Gianfranco's apartment in Florence being a mother. Gianfranco, who never explains his disappearances and appearances, keeps us all on guard but is increasingly absent. I transform minestrone into a lush, dense *ribollita* and spend dreamy half-hours up to my elbows in a vat of bright-red oily oxtail sauce, gently separating meat from bone. Gianfranco dollops a ladleful of it into another pot of simmering leek risotto, to create a masterpiece of a new dish. He chops up a box of green tomatoes, softens lots of onions in butter and bubbles the tomatoes until they become a jammy sauce, which we serve with fusilli, grating pecorino thickly over the top. He tosses Vin Santo and strawberry liqueur into the giant pan of roasting pork – the perfume is glorious – and then adds the fresh chestnuts we have all previously peeled laboriously.

On to my plate of evening spinach sautéed with lots of garlic and chilli, I drizzle some thick green olive oil, brand new, delivered that morning by Mauro. It is mid-November and nearly time for me to leave. Alvaro tells me that I seem remote, a little detached: I am not 'there in the head' and I know exactly what he means, because I have already begun the process of removing myself, readying myself for the return to such a different existence, my little flat and the usual dreary cycle of a mostly ordinary life.

In a moment of mad impulse I decide that, before returning to Australia, I must dine at the Michelin-starred Enoteca Pinchiorri in Florence and, furthermore, that I must dine there with Ignazio. I am aware that it is very expensive, but I am prepared to use my credit card: it is to be a combined birthday present to Ignazio, gesture of my affection and farewell treat to myself.

We meet as arranged in a little bar nearby. The restaurant is in the same street where we once shared an apartment, the same street where so briefly, another life ago, I had attended the Michelangelo Institute. Ignazio looks beautiful in a well-cut camel suit, his hair pomaded back, his eyes dark and dancing as he propels me through the giant iron gates and the grand, hushed entrance to the restaurant. We sit at a corner table in a room with chandeliers and stiff waiters. There is a rarefied air of luxury and *benessere* – well-being. The chairs pulled out for us by a waiter each are high-backed and solemn. There are fragrant flowers on a table busy with slender-stemmed crystal glassware arranged in neat rows and classical music murmurs.

It could almost be a scene from a play, and throughout the evening we speak in lowered tones. From the two different menus on heavy expensive paper we are handed, I whisper to Ignazio that we are obliged, for reasons of economy, to select the *menù turistico*, which offers a series of courses, without wines, for a mere 150,000 lire per head.

Entranced by everything, I feel as if every other diner there belongs to a privileged world that I have only read about and never encountered. The couple beside us who order off the standard menu and who barely speak to each other all night, he pouchy-eyed and she thin and taut, the silver teapot arriving to serve him tea with his main meal, which seems to exemplify the height of sophistication. The larger table of eight adults, whose features are chiselled and polished. The single elderly man, clearly a regular, judging by the familiarity with which he gestures to the waiter at his table, a nonchalance in the drape of the napkin, an air of bored refinement.

Each little course arriving at our table is more breathtaking than the one preceding it. We sip fizzy Müller Thurgau with the first few courses: a tumble of *alici* on *panzanella* and a dob of pesto; seared red mullet on fennel puree; potato *tortelli* with shaved white truffles. Then a soft Tignanello to accompany the pancetta-wrapped prawns on spelt; a fish soup; duck in a sticky balsamic sauce; more syrupy balsamic vinegar spooned delicately over a sublime chunk of Parmesan on a plate containing goat's cheese and poached pears; the delicate flaky apple tart with cinnamon ice cream.

We eat in a sort of trance, two waiters hovering throughout to minister to our every need, topping up wine and water, whisking away and replacing plates soundlessly, almost invisibly. With our coffee arrive two trays of unordered dessert wine and miniature pastries, biscuits and petits fours, which look like jewels, too pretty to eat, though of course we manage. The bill comes to about 500,000 lire (€260), which seems, after I have prepared myself for 600,000, to suddenly be almost ludicrously inexpensive for all we have experienced. It is easy to leave a 50,000 lire tip, the cost of a meal for two at La Cantinetta.

Afterwards, Ignazio drives me to a noisy bar on the outskirts of Florence, where we drink more and where I appal myself by eating an entire bowl of salted peanuts. Throughout the evening we have been comfortable and close, although I feel we never really talk about anything that matters. I tell him I will always love him when he eventually restores me to Spedaluzzo, before driving himself back to Scandicci.

It is my final day of work. It is cold and sunny and on my last walk the air is sharply wintry as I power along, fuelled by hurt and rage towards Alvaro, who promised to join me in my bedroom the night before, after we made fantastic love in his, and who never appeared. The complicated directions he had issued me to avoid Vito suspecting, and the trusting way I trotted off to wake alone at six o'clock, are too mortifying, too reminiscent, moreover, of Gianfranco's infidelities all those years ago. I am aware of how absurd I am being, and that the late little affair to which we robustly abandoned ourselves was as meaningless and as meaningful to both of us, but all I am feeling is that the emptiness after an affair gapes more widely than the emptiness that preceded it.

Alvaro is off to Umbria with Rita for a week; he erupts into the kitchen, where my last day is to be spent working alongside Gianfranco, and says goodbye to us, met by my wild, indifferent eyes. When he kisses me on both cheeks and says, *'Intanto ci si vede il ventisette'* – meanwhile, we'll see each other on the twenty-seventh – I wonder if he sees the faint red mark on my neck where the previous night he had bitten me and which aches from time to time with the dull, wistful longing I so absurdly feel. Another selfish uncaring bastard, and I am missing him already and immediately, and planning to buy him Zucchero's latest CD (and myself a copy to cry over), with a little card on which I will thank him for his friendship if not his sincerity.

I am hit by a wave of wild joy, suddenly, regardless of Alvaro and Vito, regardless of the surly inapproachability of Gianfranco. I am at the end of this latest round of La Cantinetta. Everything I do is imbued with the significance of being its last time. My final snack of sublime Parmesan and glass of Chianti, that most divine of marriages. Watching over the cavolo nero, beans, sausage, garlic and chilli Gianfranco has left to simmer. Even my discussion about life after death, God and religion with doddery silly-in-his-denims Vito, whose sleazy malevolence is muffled today by the lovely side of him I always used to see.

No customers at 8 p.m. and I am feeling sentimental, a little hazed by Chianti. I am looking at the neighbour who has come to borrow fondue forks, at his comical cartoon face and his beautiful, silent teenage son. Gianfranco, still in his hunting khakis, gesticulates before him and I am captured again by the beauty of eyes and mouths, gestures and whimsicalities, cigarettes lit and left drooped from casual lips: this whole mad country and its exasperating people, including Alvaro, whom I find I am missing quite violently. I have a week after this in Perugia with my beloved Raimondo and Annamaria, before returning here for a farewell dinner, then catching a train to Rome, where I will spend a final night with Marie-Claire and fly back home. Back home!

I frutti proibiti sono i più dolci
Forbidden fruit is sweetest

The dinner was not planned as a farewell for me, though coinciding with my departure as it does I decide to make it so. It is in the little castle nearby where the La Cantinetta mob gathers in a huge cold room and sits, banquet-style, in a square. I manage to find a seat near Ignazio and Alvaro and Rita, deciding I want to have fun away from the sanctity of authority and grown-up disapproval that seems to cling to Gianfranco until he has abandoned himself to drink.

Across the room I see Donatella, who has brought a female friend. They are dressed too provocatively, laugh too bawdily, but I am feeling glamorous, my hair newly bobbed and blonded by a good Perugia hairdresser, my plumpness pressed into the safety of a smart black pantsuit, my lips red. It is a lovely last night, the excellent food and wine flowing and the mood ebullient, and so it comes as an additional treat when back at La Cantinetta and preparing for bed I am interrupted by a knock on my door. It is Alvaro who has somehow managed to dispose of Rita, Alvaro who has chosen me over Rita, and immediately I dismiss all the dark thoughts I had let torture me over the previous week.

The following morning I am on the train from Florence to Rome, a compartment to myself, sliding smoothly away through bands of sunshine, Florence slipping past. I am remembering the send-off. Outside La Cantinetta, the blue SITA bus had stopped for me to clumsily negotiate my suitcase aboard and find a window seat. There they were standing in a line to wave me off, my three men – my two ex-lovers and my lover. I felt a delicious, mischievous joy at them, wanting to shout out, 'If you only knew', but waved and waved instead, until they were no longer visible.

Marie-Claire's apartment in the Trastevere has semi-restored paintings leaning against its hallway walls with dark, brooding religious scenes, centuries old. The last time I saw her was two years previously, when at the beginning of my Cantinetta stint she had brought her two children to visit their father. She reminds them who I am now. I am struck again by the resemblance of her son to Gianfranco and the beauty of her daughter, but mostly by Marie-Claire. She is dressed exquisitely, a glamorous art restorer managing, seemingly effortlessly, to combine a busy career with single motherhood, pedalling her way through the streets of Rome, dining out regularly with an assortment of boyfriends.

She takes me to a tiny *osteria* nearby, where from a generous table of antipasti we select our dishes. I notice how slowly and how little she eats – mostly vegetables and salad – and how the bread basket is emptied by me. I long to be Marie-

Claire with every pore. Meanwhile, I am regaling her with La Cantinetta stories and we are cruelly laughing, about Cinzia and Ignazio and the moodiness of Gianfranco, and I have even turned the torrid Vito business into an amusing anecdote. We drink a lot and plunge into discussions on love and sex and weight, dreams and fears. When Marie-Claire asks me why I tend to get fat when I come to Italy, I describe boredom and loneliness and lack of confidence, some great need to fill the wells of emptiness within me. I see how limp an explanation it really is, that what I essentially lack is self-discipline, resolve and inner resources; that there she is orchestrating a complicated life with two young children, a failed marriage and deep wells of her own. That maybe there is no secret after all to a successful life other than hard work and self-denial. That I am simply greedy.

I am so vastly cheered by Marie-Claire's company, so restored to my usual irreverent, humorous self, that I am already regarding the past three and a half months and the demi-monde of Spedaluzzo with affection. Melting away is the middle period of gloom and self-doubt and all I am feeling now is a sense of being loved and, after all this time, a little belonging. Still being shaped, changed and challenged by Italy, endlessly enriched and maddened by it, I am, however, now ready to go home.

Back home, my flat reclaimed, it is job searching all over again, but this time around I strike it lucky. An admiring owner of a spacious deli is so anxious that I work for her that she pays for a daily taxi to pick me up and convey me to Circular Quay, whereupon I catch the ferry across the sparkling early morning water. In the tiny kitchen at the back of the shop I toil away happily enough, working alongside women who become friends, returning in the evenings to my single life and its inevitable doses of social activity. Dinner parties and diets, restaurants and the gym: a middle-aged woman with a university degree in languages who chops up capsicums for a living.

Then two things happen. First, an old friend purchases a café and poaches me from the deli to be her chef. After three intense years beavering away there, I start hearing regularly again from my old friend William. He has moved up the coast and bought himself a house in an area I have never even visited, and he wants me to move up there as well.

'You'll love it here, Victoria,' he repeats, every single night. 'It's full of single middle-aged people like us.'

And so I do – that is the second thing. Immediately meeting his younger cousin, a beautiful artist, and falling in love.

It still takes two years of chopping up capsicums in assorted cafés and delis before realising that, as a cook in Australia, I am never going to shine, despite the Italian food I cook which everyone loves, despite the Italian cooking classes that I resume teaching to great acclaim. When the position for advertising salesperson with the local newspaper appears, I apply immediately, and am accepted. I am offered my own weekly food column shortly afterwards. Life is coming together.

Book Four

2004
San Casciano, Florence, Spedaluzzo, Perugia

La tavola e il letto mantengono l'affetto
The table and the bed keep love alive

There is a neat row of fashionable shoes – mainly pointy-toed boots – lining the hall wall of Gianfranco's bachelor flat in San Casciano. This is what I first see when I step across the threshold, although that familiar blend of just-brewed coffee, cleaning products and mustiness has already jogged me out of my jet-lagged trance. Italian apartments: the wooden shutters, the cool marble staircase, the private little arrangements of pot plants and umbrella stands outside each door, the door to unimagined spaciousness.

I am breathing it all in, standing beside my suitcase and cabin bag, and Gianfranco is already whisking ahead into his spartan kitchen to put on coffee, offer peach-flavoured iced tea and describe sleeping arrangements. Behind me is William, back in Italy after thirty years; the mere nine that have lapsed since I was here last seem, both in comparison and in reality, like weeks, puncturing the stupor of my tiredness with memories, associations and recollections.

It was Cinzia who had collected us from Rome airport some hours before. She had insisted on doing the journey from Spedaluzzo, even if it meant coming into fleeting contact at a pre-arranged meeting point with Gianfranco in order to hand us over. In her new four-wheel drive she belted out of Rome and along the autostrada at 140 kilometres per hour, mostly connected to her mobile phone, the radio roaring. Out of Lazio, up through Umbria and into the familiarity of

Tuscany she sped us, while spilling forth with the Gianfranco saga. She had thrown him out two years ago, worn down by his infidelities, his impossibility. Now she lives only for their son, Tonino, a nine-year-old, whom his father rarely sees. 'He doesn't have a father,' she mutters darkly at one point. She tells us how Gianfranco sends no money for him and helps in no way, how she has carved out a brisk, cheerful life for herself running La Cantinetta on her own with a team of only women. ('Only women!' triumphantly.) Business is good and she is happy. She has given up cigarettes and is chubby in her tight white trousers and pointy high heels – otherwise, nine years have done little to alter her.

The constant phone calls intrigue me, but I try not to tune in. I ask about various other people I know and it appears she has very little contact with any of them. She is a superwoman, she tells me several times, as she balances obsessive single motherhood with running a restaurant. I am already worn out by approving, admiring and sympathising, but put it down to jet lag – I had ended up growing fond of Cinzia all those years ago and I cannot allow her bitter view of Gianfranco, my host, my mentor, my dear friend, and my ex-boyfriend, to turn me against her. Surely…

At a layby near a roundabout, she pulls up. Some distance away I spot Gianfranco smoking a cigarette, blowing smoke out the open door of his car. Without even glancing his way, Cinzia spills us out, luggage and all, embraces us warmly, then squeals away. Gianfranco welcomes us with a hug and drives us to his apartment.

Gianfranco is exactly the same. A little stouter, a little greyer, but otherwise unchanged. He is navigating a difficult conversation in broken English and Italian with William, as I slip gratefully under the handheld shower, flooding the bathroom floor in clumsy dopey eagerness to lather the twenty-four-hour flight off me. From the liquid soap's foamy richness floats another forgotten, achingly memorable scent of my past Italian lives, beginning to unknot something that has been closed for years and years.

When I emerge, the scene is almost cosy: two middle-aged men smoking cigarettes over a confusion of pidgin English and pidgin Italian. They look relieved at being rescued by my scrubbed and gleaming entrance. Now fifty-two, Gianfranco still dresses in faded jeans and untucked denim shirts with the easy casual sexiness which first attracted me. He is telling me about the villa where he runs the kitchen of the restaurant, and has for two years since Cinzia threw him out of La Cantinetta. He and three partners took over the restaurant management of the fourteenth-century villa, which for years had been non-operational. They were slowly building it up, restoring its reputation as a venue for weddings and communions, as well as for fine dining. Gianfranco is as enthusiastic about this latest project as he has been about all the others, and yet I sense that, after the joyous autonomy of running his own restaurants, this latest one may be felt as a downhill slide.

Gianfranco wants to take us for coffee, so he is bustling us out the door into what is apparently the first sunny day in weeks and weeks. We have clearly conveyed the fine weather all the way from Australia. We drive into the centre of San Casciano. This little town I remember from a long ago visit to Paolo the dentist for some perfunctory work; Paolo, in fact, is one of Gianfranco's partners. Another partner runs the Bar Centrale, where we are ordering coffees – this is the third I have had since touching Italian soil and yet I feel I need all the caffeine I can get. We sit outside at one of the sunny little tables and presently the owner comes out to be introduced. I had forgotten Gianfranco's inability to settle for long unless late at night over wine and cigarettes, and he is already restless, issuing us rapid, complicated instructions on how to find our way back to the apartment and asking us to wake him around seven o'clock in order that we can all go out to dinner together. We are left.

William is to be with me for the first week only of this three-week stay in Italy before heading off to America. Half of me is happy to have a dear old friend to share Italy with me, and especially to be there on the day I turn fifty, but the other half is anxious. I have only ever been in Italy on my own; there is something almost sacred and deeply personal about my connection with the country and the people which I cannot explain and which I feel unable to share. Or, more honestly, which I do not want to share. The selfishness and small-mindedness of the realisation shocks me. Complete re-immersion is what I am planning in this snatched return, because I have come with the hope of making sense of it all. I need confirmation that over the years I have not embroidered and embellished, invented and fabricated, forgotten or exaggerated: I need to find out if it was real.

Esse nufesso chi dice male di macaruni
He who speaks badly of macaroni is a fool

That first night Gianfranco takes us to dinner at Nello restaurant. We are joined by Paolo the dentist and his wife. I am enchanted by the company, despite being a little worried that in my jet-lagged state, and after so many years away, my Italian will be rough, if accessible at all. I always loved Paolo and Silvana, a couple intriguingly contrasted; Paolo a short, fierce-eyed man with a limp alongside tall, black, beautiful Silvana. We move into the busy restaurant, where the celebrity treatment, which always seems to accompany dining out with Gianfranco, begins immediately. Within minutes, food and wine have arrived on the table, platters of *bresaola* and moist lush prosciutto, salamis and mortadellas, crostini with assorted toppings, baskets of bread, the Chianti poured.

William, at the end of the table, is eating too much of everything and tossing back wine, and as the evening progresses, somehow dredging up half-forgotten Italian and managing more or less to keep pace. I am flushed, excited, tongue loosened, too, by the wine and talking nonstop, then remembering to eat. Food continues to arrive in the form of garlicky roast green tomatoes, rare roast beef slices so tender they barely require cutting, a multi-flavoured *spezzatino* or casserole, whole porcini mushrooms roasted with herbs and garlic. Gianfranco sits at the head becoming progressively louder and more entertaining.

William, a hyperbolic man under normal circumstances, is proclaiming it the best meal he has ever eaten in his life and I observe with relief that his excessive behaviour is striking just the right note with everyone else at the table. When cigarettes are lit with flagrant disregard of the various no-smoking signs around the dining room, I can see how beautifully he is fitting in and that I do not need to worry about him. And, to be sure, it is William who is still drinking liqueurs back at the apartment of Paolo and Silvana where we retreat after dinner, carrying on semi-coherent conversations with Gianfranco and Paolo as I feel myself slipping further and further down my chair. There is nothing to worry about with William.

Back at Gianfranco's I leave the two of them, William and Gianfranco, still engaged in animated conversation as I wash my face and clean my teeth. Periodically William calls out, 'What's the word for energy?' or 'How do you say "spiritual"?' to which I am too tired, too full and too drunk to reply. We have twin beds in a spare bedroom belonging to Gianfranco's teenage children, when they come from Paris to stay with him. Earlier Gianfranco had drawn me aside and asked if I was happy with this arrangement. Because, if I wasn't, he went on, I could sleep in his room. There was nothing lascivious in the offer and yet it made me wonder what he would have expected had I agreed. The last two times I saw Gianfranco there was a noticeable absence of sexual frisson between us; rather, there was a sense of something deeper and richer and better, and I have been aware of this same solidity since we arrived. He was just being, I imagine, his thoughtful and considerate self.

After the sunny May day when we arrive, the weather returns to unseasonable awfulness: it rains constantly, it is windy and cold, and one night it hails so heavily that on my morning walk the following day I crunch through brittle white ice like snow. This, combined with the several days it seems to take to recover from jet lag, shifts my focus from lofty thoughts to feeling comfortable.

I am in Italy on holiday. I am not here to work, unlike the previous two trips. I have three entire weeks, most of which will be spent as a guest of Gianfranco, with the remainder in Perugia with Raimondo. I am here to turn fifty, because I happened to be in Italy for those other two milestones, forty and thirty. I am also here to absorb the food scene in order to fill more evocatively my weekly columns for the local newspaper where I work. I am here because I have left it too long to return to a place and to people responsible for shaping my life so dramatically. I am sharply conscious, moreover, of coming back into this world a woman infinitely more at ease and at peace with herself than at any other time. I even mostly like myself.

The next day, Gianfranco takes us to look at the villa. It confounds me, its warrens and entrances and dining rooms and staircases, its sudden little sitting rooms and archways and secret gardens. It dates from the fourteenth century and one of the rooms is still filled with furniture from that era. Several apartments are out of bounds, belonging to and constituting the home of an elderly family member; the rest of it is at the disposal of Gianfranco and his partners.

The kitchen is enormous and the dining room gracious, formal and polite. There is an arbour outside, long tables under the arch of creeping vines where I imagine sitting until midnight on languid summer nights. Around the panels of one room are black-and-white photographs of dignitaries and celebrities coming to dine in the 1940s and 1950s. There is a very young Elizabeth Taylor and a youthful, dashing Shah of Persia. The grounds are glorious, with their beautifully manicured garden beds, fountains, statuary and huge ceramic urns of lemons trees.

A wash of pride towards Gianfranco briefly suffuses me: the talent he has for finding the most beautiful restaurants in which to work. I am also seeing how much more grandiose an operation this is than any he has undertaken previously. The huge kitchen, for example, accommodates three chefs, including himself. Most of their work so far comes from wedding and communion parties of over a hundred people at a time.

Standing in the middle of that enormous kitchen, I find myself feeling perfectly at home. The familiar low, wide pans containing simmering sauces invite me to give an occasional stir to their contents, and so I do, an instinct, the wooden spoon dipping through the unctuousness of a dark rich ragout, a peppery beef stew. Gianfranco's second chef is a tall beautiful Albanian youth, who clears away stainless-steel bench space for me to set up my cheesecake-making paraphernalia; I can't resist the opportunity to cook. The other chef is short, wiry and florid, and for a while the three of us dance around each other clumsily and politely as we establish our territories.

Chocolate-hazelnut cheesecake

*Toast 3 handfuls of hazelnuts until golden, then rub
off as many skins as come away easily. Set aside.*

Crust
*In a food processor, grind 250 g digestive biscuits to
crumbs. Melt 85 g butter and add to biscuit crumbs together
with 2 tablespoons caster sugar. Mix well and press into
a greased spring-form pan. Chill while you make the
filling. Preheat oven to 150°C (300°F, Gas mark 2).*

Filling
*In a large bowl, add 150g (2/3 cup) of caster sugar to 600g
softened cream cheese and blend well. Add 1 teaspoon of
vanilla essence, then 3 eggs, one at a time, beating well after
each addition. Coarsely chop the hazelnuts. Coarsely chop
150 g dark cooking chocolate, then fold through cheesecake
mix together with two-thirds of the nuts. Pour into crumb
crust and bake for about an hour or until set. Allow to cool.
In a double boiler, melt 100 g of dark cooking chocolate.
Scatter remaining nuts over cheesecake, then drizzle melted
chocolate over the top. Chill at least an hour before serving.*

I am excited about seeing Ignazio. I had been told how he, too, had left La Cantinetta, met a woman, had a baby, bought a restaurant. Within two years, everything collapsed and so now here he is being waiter for Gianfranco all over again, single father of an eight-year-old daughter he sees twice a week. It is not lost on me the extraordinary coincidence of the three of us being together again a decade since the last time, as if we had been one smooth, untrammelled trio all along – something meant by it all.

I hear his voice before I see him – and there he is, hair gelled back into a sharp peak, the same beautiful face I remember, the short compact body a little heavier. We hug tightly and I stand back: was his face always so spectrally white? Gianfranco has murmured mentions of drinking and gambling problems, and to be sure there seems to be a ruined beauty around my Botticelli angel. I always loved the way I could stand eye level to Ignazio and wrap my arms around his neck and we fit so neatly. I love this still. He makes us both an espresso from the coffee machine, which we gulp down, and then I am back to the cheesecake and Ignazio is clicking off to set tables. Smoothing the lemon cream filling onto the crumbed base, I have the strange sensation of never having left Italy at all, as if I am taking up precisely and seamlessly where I left off, like the trick photography that imposes a new entity within the outlines of the old. I have returned to my Italian persona.

Into our midst explodes Gianfranco at his most baggy-eyed, early morning dissolute, barking out instructions to his chefs, stabbing numbers on his mobile phone, cigarette between his lips and the coffee grinder roaring. I slide the cake into the massive oven a little anxiously – Gianfranco has told me that the temperature controls are dubious – and take off to one of the dining rooms to study the menu while I wait for it to cook. Did I ever leave?

Ciò che si mangia con gusto non fa mai male
What you eat with pleasure
can never make you ill

Within three days my Italian has returned in torrents. William and I set out early each morning from San Casciano to catch a bus somewhere. It is mostly to Florence, except for one wet day, to San Gimignano, where we join convoys of tourists and squealing school excursions under a canopy of umbrellas. I rediscover the little piazza where eleven years ago I had listened, entranced, to a German flautist ripple through his repertoire, but I am disenchanted by the beautiful old town's determined pursuit of tourism.

Florence that first day threatens to be as disappointing. It is cold and wet and only barely May, so why these throngs of tourists? I charge ahead of William and lose him periodically. I want to feel moved, and nothing happens. Is it over-familiarity? Why is my heart not swelling? Everything begins to irritate me, from the buffeting crowds to the haughty waiters whose frosty disdain I do not remember. I pine for the lira, money whose value I understand, rather than the euro; it seems to me that everything has become inordinately expensive.

Several nights we dine at the villa. This means filling in time till ten o'clock at night, when the preparation begins for the staff meal, which we are joining. There are few customers at this time of year and the process of becoming known is long and slow. The vast imperious dining rooms seem too lofty, too cold for the two or three tables of diners, and Ignazio in bow tie carving meat from a trolley looks stilted, anachronistic, in all that emptiness.

When it comes time to eat, I have to force myself to slow down. I want to try everything on the table. There is soft, sweet pecorino cheese cut into wedges to accompany fresh broad beans, marinated artichoke hearts in their pool of green oil, Gianfranco's heavenly *peposa*, a peppery beef casserole he used to make at La Cantinetta, a chunk of spicy salami to wrap inside the gorgeous, spongy hard-crusted bread which I am never able to resist.

Other nights, Gianfranco drives William and me into Florence for dinner. We arrive late at noisy pizzerias in the centre of town and are naturally whisked to the best table and plied immediately with food and wine. I am remembering his habit of surly taciturnity at the beginnings of meals, when he is concentrating on eating, filling his wine glass several times over with mineral water, and only seeming to cheer up when he has finished eating, extracted a cigarette, splashed out wine.

Peposa all'Imprunetana
(Pepper beef, Impruneta style)

Heat olive oil in a heavy pot with several peeled cloves of garlic and some rosemary sprigs, and brown 1 kg of diced blade steak in batches until brown all over. Add 2 stalks of finely chopped celery and 1 large red onion, finely chopped, together with 2 tablespoons whole black peppercorns, freshly and coarsely crushed. (Place under tea towel and pound with meat mallet.) After about 20 minutes, slosh in 1 cup of red wine and bring to the boil, then simmer until wine has evaporated. Add 400 g of peeled tomatoes, extra water and salt to taste. Bring back to the boil, then simmer for 1 1/2 to 2 hours – or until meat is very tender.

That first week is wet, cold and windy; outside each front door on every marbled level of Gianfranco's building are crowded umbrella stands. We dry our underwear on the column heaters and I am obliged to borrow a stylish blissfully cosy cardigan from Gianfranco, who has already issued me with a spare mobile phone. Everyone is using them constantly, flicking back the tiny covers with unconscious grace.

I had expected to celebrate my birthday night at the villa, with visions of being fussed over and spoiled by ex-boyfriends and new friends. As it turned out, a wedding and two communion parties were booked for that date, so William organises a table at Nello restaurant, which had so enraptured us on our first night. Gianfranco is anxious that after dinner we come to the villa for cake and spumante.

Nello is an experience utterly unlike the first night – I feel it the second we are led to our table by the waiter. In the brightly lit buzzy dining room, it seems we are the only non-Italians, the sole *stranieri*. Without Gianfranco I am trying to improvise, unsure what to choose from the menu, chattering too brightly to the haughty distant waiter. I suppress my irritation with everything – with the waiter, with William for drinking too quickly, but above all with the fact that on this special occasion the situation is just William and I exhibiting our standard greed and not even particularly enjoying our meal.

We choose badly – my pheasant is dry, William's lamb a little tough – and even the three types of crostini we order for the beginning are less luscious than they were that first night. I conclude privately that it is less to do with the absence of Gianfranco than with my state of mind. I had so wanted a special, fancy, unforgettable birthday dinner, even if it were to be just the two of us bravely celebrating. There is a candle on my cheese platter, a redeeming touch, and then the owner insists on driving us to the villa, where the final guests are departing and the cleaning up is taking place.

In the end dining room, exhausted waiters are setting up for the staff dinner. Gianfranco is already seated and engrossed in podding broad beans, smoking ashtray at his elbow. We slide in at the long table, and in dribs and drabs the rest arrive to settle into the leisurely business of eating and drinking. Ignazio, shirt tails flapping and bow tie discarded, brings out a bottle of the Cartizze Gianfranco promised me the day we arrived, flutes are filled and a huge chocolate cake brought to the table with a spitting sizzling sparkler on top. Everyone sings *'Tanti auguri a te, tanti auguri a te, tanti auguri a Veeky, tanti auguri a te'* and I could weep at the loveliness of it all.

The following day, grey and moist, Paolo, Silvana and I drive William into Florence to catch the train to Rome. I stand on the platform smiling fiercely at the windowed face of this exasperating, beloved friend of mine who I am suddenly missing, even before the train has pulled out. Then he is gone, and I am still standing there on the rapidly emptying platform, aware of a swelling of such freedom and possibility that I am for a moment frozen. Where do I begin? Two entire weeks of Italy, the keys to Gianfranco's mostly vacant apartment a bus ride away, a smart mobile phone, old friends to seek out or surprise, and old stamping grounds to recover.

Silvana and I begin at the little San Casciano market held every Monday near the main bus stop. Stalls create three aisles of shopping along the ridge whose dramatic drop throws up a vision of almost clichéd Tuscan countryside. I trail behind Silvana, who knows most of the stallholders, haggling, joking and filling her jewelled fingers with carrier bags in the process.

Sunlight is splintering stubbornly through the damp fuggy air, the first real sun I have seen since the day we arrived. I need everything and nothing. I dither over a pair of shoes I like, but when Silvana urges me to buy them, I change my mind. She has bought underwear, two sets of bedlinen and three boxes of shoes, and is now selecting Parmesan from the mobile cheese van. The food aisle features several of these makeshift delicatessens and I plant myself in front of each, absorbing sights and smells and enjoying the lively bargaining taking place around me. Huge wedges of several types of Parmesan, wheels of pecorino, both aged and sweet, fat plaits of creamy white mozzarella, blocks of Gorgonzola, goat's cheeses, pale craterous Emmentals: this is my vision of heaven. Alongside are cured meats, haunches of prosciutto, giant mortadellas and tiny crinkled sausages and salamis, and a whole roasted suckling pig sliced through its gorgeous lacquered coat.

Behind me I can hear Silvana's laughter peel out across the morning. I turn and watch her joke with the greengrocer, whose fingers are testing asparagus spears for firmness. Glossy zucchini and broad beans and artichoke hearts nestle alongside mangetout and green beans, aubergine and capsicum, four varieties of tomato, frilly lettuces, fat globes of fennel, bunches of celery, pert little radishes – produce so fresh I can almost hear it squeak. Silvana is now gathering me up, thrusting carrier bags into my arms, organising to meet me outside Nello at half past twelve so I can join her and Paolo for lunch.

I order a salad, Silvana, crostini and prosciutto followed by chicken; and Paolo, grilled liver. He pulls bread apart absently and reminisces about the bachelor period in his life when he sat at the same table of Nello every single day until Silvana came into his life. The talk turns to Cinzia, the only woman Gianfranco had been involved with whom he did not betray. Yet she believed that he did, terminated the relationship, somehow wrested the restaurant from his control, took it over and eventually bought out the last remaining partner.

Paolo and Silvana do not hide their contempt for her. I listen carefully and insert occasional questions. There is still much I fail to comprehend. How could she throw him out of a restaurant of his own inception, a restaurant so successful that there would be queues of people waiting to get in? How could she ensure that he received nothing at all for everything he had done? There seems no justification for such a cruel act of revenge. Paolo tells me how Gianfranco slunk away for six months to lie low, barely seeing anyone. Then the opportunity of the villa arose.

La Cantinetta is now a mere half the restaurant it once was, and mostly panders to tourists. I ask desultory questions about Gianfranco's love life, the string of women

218

– mostly foreigners – who fall in love with him and whom he drops with regularity. The only time Gianfranco and I are really alone in the ten days I am his guest is when we go to the Metro, the vast wholesale emporium on the outskirts of Florence. When he was teaching me how to cook, we used to go regularly on shopping trips that were the stuff of fantasy and spend extravagant amounts.

This experience is both the same and different – twenty years separate us from the two people we once were. When we arrive, we procure one of the huge, ungainly trolleys and proceed up and down the aisles, me pushing and Gianfranco loading. Rounding a corner into an aisle of tropical fruits and punnets of multicoloured berries, we are suddenly standing face to face with a man so familiar, whose mouth splits into a wide smile of pleasure as he says, 'How lovely to see you both!'. We chat for several minutes, then move on and I hiss to Gianfranco that I do not remember who it is. 'Neither do I!' he laughs. We both laugh. Afterwards I do remember his name and recall that he was a waiter at a restaurant we frequented, but it must have looked for all the world as if Gianfranco and I had been together all these years in one unbroken thread.

Being with Gianfranco this time is so comfortable, it is almost familial. Here we simply are, devoid of any of the tensions associated with sex and work, two grown-ups connected by such a fond mesh of our younger, sillier selves. It is not that I find him unattractive – dressed up as he was on the first night in smart black trousers and flowing white shirt and polished pointy boots, he was meltingly lovely – it is that I know him too well, and so the nature of the chemistry has altered. During the course of the journey, he has become enthusiastic about ways to extricate me from my ongoing impecuniousness, computes with speedy calculations how a little business of private catering could rescue me, reels off simple menus, the ideas tumbling out in his lazy Umbrian accent, the cigarette waving circles above the steering wheel. The man becoming passionate fleetingly, then losing interest, distracted quickly, but the mind, like an overexcited heart, almost audibly hammering out the rhythm of rapid thought.

Quando la pera è matura, casca da sè
All things happen in their own good time

Meanwhile, I am re-establishing contact with other people. The day William leaves I find my way down to the villa, earlier than usual, a book to keep me company. I walk into the back dining room, which to my surprise contains tables and diners, and there at the head of one is Fabio, our jack of all trades from La Cantinetta. I am enchanted and swoop into his embrace. I always loved this big bear of a man and I would periodically meet his English partner, Lidia, in Florence for coffee. Lidia is there, as well, talking with a couple I dimly recognise; a chair is pulled out for me, wine splashed into a glass, a wheel of fresh, bulgy pecorino cheese and a basket of broad beans pushed in my direction.

At a corner table sit three girls whose peals of laughter pierce the formality of the gracious room with its high

ceilings and vast mirrors. Around an ice bucket they are
waving their champagne flutes with animated gestures
and blowing out ribbons of smoke. Lidia whispers that
they are call girls from Moldavia, and suddenly the
periodic visits to their table by the waiters and Gianfranco
make sense. Beppe, in his bright waiter's shirt, has seated
himself at their table: it has now become a compelling
piece of theatre. Lank-haired Gianfranco has emerged
from the kitchen, stomach sculptured into a globe by
apron strings. He leans over our table, graciously hosting,
before joining the call girls' table, to which my eyes drift
back.

There is Ignazio with more champagne, a battery of
glassware threaded through his fingers and a bow tie
slipped around his unbuttoned collar, and Gianfranco
is sitting down beside the quieter and plainer of the
girls. I am only half concentrating on the conversation
at our table – which has drifted now to that universal
fascination, the price of real estate.

These girls intrigue me, with their hipless exotic
exhibitionism; one is now dancing slow motion to her
reflection in one of the vast wall mirrors. Platters of food
remain untouched around them, and one by one the
waiters are pulling up chairs and joining in. Silvana and
Paolo are settling at another table and beginning their
own meal. The kitchen is closing down. I sit on at my
table, conscious of how staidly middle-aged we all are,
of flickers of wistfulness that I am not part of that other
infinitely more exciting party, a pretty young thing in my
twenties with an audience of admiring men.

On one of my trips into Florence, I go searching for my old restaurant. I locate Via della Condotta and the nearby Chinese restaurant, but I am confused by these fashionable new eateries that have sprung up since I was last there. Eventually I am obliged to ask about it. The first place draws a blank, but in the second funky Japanese-themed restaurant a waiter appears old enough to remember. It has had a name change, I am told; sure enough, when I retrace my steps, there is a familiar threshold and, inside, the bar area is immediately recognisable.

In contrast, I could have found with my eyes closed the cellar-restaurant where I first met Gianfranco. I descend the steps and am struck by the sharp memories and the potent image of myself perched at a typewriter on the first level doing the daily wine lists. Further in, the warm space envelops me, and there is the owner, hair now tipped a distinguished grey and wearing fashionable glasses, coming to hug me tightly. Because I am eager to catch Sant'Ambrogio markets before they close, I only stay for a few minutes, promising to return for lunch at a later stage. As I leave, I am asked if I still make my famous cheesecakes. 'But of course!' I smile. 'I made one yesterday for Gianfranco.'

I love the little Sant'Ambrogio markets and yet I have never located them with ease. They are in the Santa Croce end of town, a part of Florence that seems untroubled by tourists. I enjoy the getting lost, the chancing upon little back and side streets and *erboriste* and bookbinding shops, which have probably been operating since the sixteenth century. Nearly everywhere I go in Florence brings back a certain period of my Italian life. This particular area resonates with the snug existence Ignazio and I spun together in our Via Ghibellina apartment, of the dark winter evening when I discovered I was pregnant.

Then there is the Institute where I enrolled to do my course in Italian before meeting Gianfranco. And later, when I was extravagant and took Ignazio to dinner at the Enoteca Pinchiorri. I pass the barber shop where I ran that morning when the shower water inexplicably stopped as I was massaging conditioner into my hair. And there is the corner bar whose barista always designed perfect hearts in the cream of my cappuccino. Here, finally, is the beginning of the market. Stalls and trestle tables run neatly up both sides of a pavilion which houses the cheeses, breads, small goods, meats and poultry. It is here I have come to find Antonella and her brother and their cheese shop.

We all see each other at the same time. Their matching brown eyes widen in surprise, and then pleasure, and we rush to embrace. They are wearing white smocks. Carlo's hair is tipped with grey and Antonella looks strikingly beautiful, like her mother. We are all talking at the same time, but somehow the information is conveyed: Cesare is well but in jail, Antonella has hooked up with Carlo's oldest friend, they both have teenage children. We marvel at the passage of time, at the fact that everything changes, and at the end we agree to meet for dinner at the villa in several days' time. I do not ask why Cesare is in jail. I remember how tall he was, how his black lustrous hair flowed down his back, his impenetrable eyes and missing teeth and a sort of showy Sicilian arrogance. It was bound to have been drugs.

Tale il padre, tale il figlio
Like father, like son

One morning I am in the villa kitchen locating the various bits of equipment I require for cheesecake baking, slipping soundlessly between the chefs and taking small sips from an espresso Ignazio has made for me, when a voice I know well roars greetings from the passageway. We are all surprised. Giorgio Sabatini, son of my old friends Vincenzo and Claudia, is standing in the doorway, his face breaking into a broad grin as he enfolds me in his bear-like arms. He has become so like his father that I almost expect to see him dressed in the same enormous denim overalls dear Vincenzo habitually wore. Instead he is speaking to me in his softly accented American English, telling me how happy he is to see me.

Giorgio and his friend Pete are in Italy briefly, mainly to visit Giorgio's mother. Vincenzo had died the previous year – it seemed incredible that life could be extinguished from that robustness, from such a hearty appetite for living. Claudia and Vincenzo had been so tremendously loving and supportive of me throughout the tortured phases of Gianfranco. The times I had stayed with them had been reminiscent of time spent as a very young child at my grandparents' place. My afternoons spent drinking home-made wine and grappa with Vincenzo and eating Claudia's exquisite biscotti while we discussed life issues constituted tracts of happiness in a period otherwise fraught, anxious and lonely. And Giorgio, as ebullient and generous as his parents, I had always adored as well.

He is splashing Vernaccia into a wine glass, draping prosciutto onto chunks of bread, talking, eating and drinking all at the same time. Not only did he lose his father, but also his lovely American wife – the reason he moved to Florida where he still resides – the mother of two teenage daughters he now rears on his own. And yet he is asking me about my life, pouring more wine, preparing another sandwich, laughing with Pete and joking with Ignazio, his exuberance spreading throughout the kitchen. He has come to take delivery of Gianfranco's sports car, which up until this moment I had not known existed. With customary magnanimousness, Gianfranco is lending Giorgio and Pete the car for the several days they will spend in Tuscany.

And thus, two hours later when the cheesecake has been extracted from the oven and Giorgio and Pete have finished sitting under the pergola eating pasta and drinking more wine, I am climbing into the car with both of them, bound for San Gimignano. This is the sort of spontaneous, unexpected behaviour I rarely permit myself: a heady risk-taking quality I find both terrifying and liberating. I feel San Gimignano is a little wasted on me, having explored it that damp day a week previously with William, but Pete has not been there, so down the autostrada we tear, discussing politics and war.

We do not end up in San Gimignano anyway. Suddenly, Giorgio decides it is Certaldo that he would rather show us. The Renault curls and coils up winding roads until we arrive at the base of this medieval hill town. We park and proceed on foot, stopping at bars for shots of Vernaccia to fortify our climb to the little castle at the very top. A girl in a long black dress is sitting on a stool singing Renaissance songs, her long fingers sweeping across the strings of a harp. I stop, transfixed by the scene. Here, in this soft moist afternoon with the infinite powder-grey sky rolling across the fields, the courtyards and cool stone passageways and staircases of the castle, this fragile music playing to a handful of people in a timeless ancient town, I feel churning in me a sharp hot joy, a blend of being blessed and being lucky. We sit for a long time listening to the music, and then we explore the castle and take photos.

We return to the car via another visit to another bar, and then we are off again, streaking through a countryside turning dark with dusk. We end up at Artimino, a gracious and glorious restaurant in another hill town, where I had been taken years before by Gianfranco. Giorgio is greeted like royalty by the maître d', who sweeps us to a table and brings us spumante and menus. We dine richly and extravagantly, and we drink a lot. Giorgio insists on paying for everything, before setting off on the long journey back to San Casciano to deposit me home.

There is a moment when Pete had gone for a walk to digest, somewhat, our lavish feast, and Giorgio is reminding me of the morning he came to visit me in the little Osteria del Guanto apartment where Gianfranco and I were living at the time. As soon as he begins the memory, I know exactly what he is talking about, a morning after a night when Gianfranco had failed to come home at all and I had spent the night sleepless and sick with worry. When Giorgio arrived, I simply poured it all out. It was the first time we had ever had an intimate, confiding conversation. I was so bruised and fragile, it was the only sort I could manage. I had not forgotten it – Giorgio's infinite gentleness, his explaining about Gianfranco's impossible character, his soothing smoothing over. And he has never forgotten it, either. I am enchanted by the significance with which we have both endowed it, and deeply touched. Giorgio also tells me repeatedly how seeing me this time has been so wonderful and somehow made more sense of this particular visit to Italy for him, a little serendipity. Of course, I feel that, too.

Silvana and I are in Florence, doing the stores. We have barely been off the bus and she is already wheeling me into designer shoe shops, already slipping her small high-arched feet into teetering stilettos. I am wishing I had dressed more smartly; beside Silvana, I always feel somehow drab and homespun, especially when I observe the deference with which the male shop assistants attend to her. She looks so expensive, too, in her short silk jacket and tapered, tailored trousers and her jingling gold jewellery. She settles on two pairs of shoes and we are off, bustling along the narrow footpath that leads into the centre, stopping frequently so she can point out a pleasing window display.

I am already sick of hearing my voice offering up a range of variations on the theme of *'sì, è bellissimo'* and privately wondering if, after all, an afternoon spent watching Silvana buy shoes will be much fun. She whisks me into her favourite dress shop and I feel the fabrics flutter insubstantially between my fingers while I digest the prices. And this is only the beginning – she wants to cover Via delle Belle Donne and Via Tornabuoni, two of the most expensive streets in Florence, and so I abandon myself to fantasy, soon becoming inured to trousers which cost the equivalent of a small car, evening dresses worth more than my annual salary. After a while, a skirt costing almost €700 seems like a bargain. We walk for miles, miles, miles, and Silvana's collection of carrier bags increases while my solitary one contains a bottle of contact lens solution and a packet of arty postcards to send home.

Eventually we collapse into chairs at Giubbe Rosse in the Piazza della Repubblica. Waiters materialise immediately and hover around Silvana with menus. She orders tea and I a glass of wine, and we sit for half an hour as the evening creeps in. We have arranged to meet Gianfranco and Paolo for dinner at a seafood restaurant called Vittoria and, when we feel we have recovered a little energy, we set off again.

We are early, already settling in at a large round table in the formal, brightly lit dining room, when in limps Paolo. A little later, Gianfranco arrives and introduces Nadia, the dark-haired woman he had been sitting beside at the table of Moldavian call girls the previous week. Silvana and I nudge each other under the table; we whisper that she does not look a day over eighteen. Yet there is Gianfranco solicitously steering her into a chair, his hand on her knee, explaining something to her, lighting her cigarette. Cigarettes are about all Nadia consumes throughout the evening.

The festive process has begun, platter after platter of seafood dishes brought to our table, presumably ordered by Gianfranco, but Nadia is not eating any of it. She is sipping a Coca-Cola and I am conscious, suddenly, of how relaxed and ebullient I am. I am shrieking with laughter at something Silvana is telling me and serving myself too quickly. I feel flushed and jolly, a sharp contrast to Nadia, who barely speaks, whose face keeps lapsing into sullenness. I have asked her several questions about herself – where she is from, how long she has been in Italy – and noted how limited her Italian is, which only reinforces my increasing sense of confidence. At a certain point – at the insistence of Gianfranco – a special plate of chargrilled hunks of bread, snowy mozzarella balls and sliced tomato appears for the woman in the seafood restaurant who will not eat seafood. Nadia toys with it, lights another cigarette, smiles bravely at Gianfranco, carves off a small portion, and sips her Coke.

And there in a rush I recognise her. I see myself twenty-two years ago, sitting beside a man with whom I am utterly, blindly in love, and all around me swirls vibrant conversation I can barely grasp and my stomach has closed to the prospect of food. I am in love and prepared to put up with everything which is incomprehensible and difficult, not least the boisterous, exuberant man beside me who has already tired of ensuring I am entertained and happy. I see how far I have travelled, and how much I pity her, Nadia, the journey ahead.

Non si può cavar sangue da una rapa
You can't get blood out of a stone

The days of my unstructured holiday fill quickly, most of them involving reunions. But I miss those I can no longer meet, the friends whose deaths I heard about over the years (the magnificent Emba and her son Maurizio, Vincenzo Sabatini, Ignazio's mother, and Annamaria, most tragically, of a heart attack, far too young) and those whose lives have led them elsewhere. I meet with Ignazio's sister Pamela, and over coffee in an Irish pub I tell her about my life in a fashionable seaside town, my job at the newspaper, the man I love and the cooking classes I teach. She tells me about Ignazio, about the woman he hooked up with and never married, but with whom he attempted an ordinary family life when the baby girl was born; about the restaurant he set up with a friend, the financial struggles, the gambling, his open-heartedness, which resulted in hordes of friends turning up most evenings to eat and drink away the profits, and the ultimate betrayal by the so-called friend leading to the final fizzing failure. Now Ignazio is alone in a farmhouse at Figline with weekly access to the daughter he loves more than anything else in the world.

We marvel at the shame and the waste of it all, then head off to the markets to browse through stalls where I find the pink floral jacket I have been searching for all week – every woman, it seems, is wearing a floral jacket – and to end up drinking wine together at a little bar near the station before my bus back home. I wrap my arms around her, this sweet lively girl, my somehow sister-in-law, and before I step onto the bus we promise to send each other emails.

Another morning, Leo, one of Gianfranco's friends, picks me up from outside the villa to whisk me off for lunch. His Mexican wife Maria has been so long in Italy now that she seems more Italian than Mexican. She serves us home-made tagliatelle in a creamy smoked salmon sauce, then large bowls of *seppie in inzimino*, fleshy rings of tender calamari in garlicky spinach, into which we dip crunchy oily *fettunta*. Leo brings a cut-glass decanter of amber liquid, which he splashes into tiny glasses. 'Just sip it slowly,' he says, twinkling at me. I do, and my mouth nearly explodes with the heat of a hundred hot chillies, while he and Maria look on, laugh, and proceed to relate stories about the various guests they have shocked with Leo's home-made chilli-infused grappa.

Cinzia, who seemed so keen that we spend at least one evening together that first day she picked me up from the airport, has already changed our appointment several times. It appears that, not only is she the world's busiest woman, but that there may also be a man involved. We finally arrange that I catch the bus to Spedaluzzo several days before leaving Tuscany; she will drive me back to San Casciano afterwards. I am eager to revisit La Cantinetta – firstly for nostalgia, and secondly to see how she has changed it.

All the conversations since arriving have presented different versions of what happened between Cinzia and Gianfranco, the downfall of their partnership, the demise of a once-successful and popular restaurant, so I am unable to believe any one. Each version seems more a reflection of loyalty to one party or the other; knowing both Cinzia and Gianfranco, I find it impossible to see guiltlessness at all and instead feel, privately, that they both may have got what they deserved.

The bus trip past the lush Ugolino golf course and threading through the little villages is all so well-worn that the sharp stabs of nostalgia I expect do not come; then I get off outside the big old building at Spedaluzzo with a move as slick as instinct and my heart lurches in recognition.

From outside all appears as before, and then I move through the heavy wrought-iron gates and crunch across the gravelly forecourt that leads to the outdoor dining areas and turn left into the kitchen.

There is Cinzia, grinning at me from a table of customers she is serving, her arms clutching big menus, and then wobbling to greet me on high wedge heels. She assures me lunch is nearly over and she will be able to sit with me soon – meanwhile, I must meet her kitchen staff.

And so I am ushered into the building and through to a kitchen so much smaller and darker than I remembered that I am briefly thrown out. Did we really manage all those communions and weddings and boisterous summer groups from that tiny space? Cinzia had told me, breathlessly, how well they work together now that it is just women ('*solo donne!*'). And yet I am remembering the dynamic there used to be between Gianfranco and me, then Alvaro and me, between the three of us, and recognise retrospectively a uniqueness we possessed as a kitchen team, in spite of all the tensions, tempers and the tantrums, the heavy drinking and the private dramas – or even because of all of these.

Back outside is the little covered area like a greenhouse that I always loved, although a brick fireplace has replaced what used to be Ignazio's bar, sealing off the ghosts of swirling wide-hipped Brazilian girls, that joyous music and molten energy. The upper area is as lovely as ever; there are only two tables in the sun, occupied by late lunchers. Then there is the cabana-style section further up where we used to park the trolley mid-centre, the showpiece for our artistically arranged prosciuttos and whole pecorinos and breads and baked ricottas studded with rocket and my beautiful desserts and straw-wrapped flasks of Chianti. The area next to that, however – which all summer used to pulsate with buzzy crowds of bronzed partying customers – now has an air of neglect, the paint peeling off the wooden tables, the chairs upturned.

Glass of wine in hand, I am studying the menu while Cinzia bustles around gathering empty bottles. The menu is mostly how I remember it, retaining many of Gianfranco's signature dishes. There are now, however, English translations and Cinzia's are highly amusing.

'Do you want me to correct this?' I call out at one point, referring to 'in the house-made virgin olive oil, pickles, and Antishocks'. Gianfranco's *tagliate* are still featured: simply grilled, sublimely flavoured *Chianina* beef served sliced on the diagonal and adorned with assorted toppings – but there was never a *tagliata esotica* described as 'Sliced Deboned Steak with Avocado and Goat's Cheese'. Here is Cinzia at my elbow telling me how popular with the *stranieri* the restaurant has become, when I would have thought that success with Florentines would have been preferable.

She has brought me a slice of 'cannamon cake' made by a woman she knows. When I look blank, she says it is made with '*cannella*'. 'Oh! It's a cinnamon cake,' I correct her, then am surprised by how lovely it is, moist and cinnamony with thick cream on the top and in the middle, but I only eat a little of it, because I am being taken out to dinner later by Ignazio.

Cinzia never manages to settle down with me, being the super mamma she is; running a restaurant and looking after her son means that she is constantly moving. We are to go to pick up Tonino now from school. She is stepping out of one pair of trousers and into another and telling me about the man she is seeing. I wonder if she is making too much about the timing here, ensuring that I am aware that her affair began respectably beyond the break-up with Gianfranco. I am beset with a sense of not knowing what is truth, or whom to believe. I just listen, and respond sympathetically, and then we drive off in her unwieldy four-wheel drive.

Seeing Tonino brings a blend of shock and sadness. No one has prepared me for how fat he is. He is hanging around an emptied classroom when we arrive, and then flops against his mother, resentfully. I am overly bright to him when introduced, but he seems bored, restless, unimpressed by my exotic Australian-ness and I stifle my dislike. This is Gianfranco's baby! This is the fruit of his union with Cinzia, and I am vainly, surreptitiously, trying to find his father in all that fleshiness, those flinty narrow eyes. I sit back in the car and allow the conversation to flow around me, Cinzia softening Tonino's petulance with her musical voice, as caressing as a lover's.

When we reach San Casciano, she has caved in to his insistence that they go and visit papa. We park the car and proceed on foot, stopping at a greengrocer to buy cherries. I suddenly want to have a photo of Tonino holding the cherries and ask him to pose for me. He stands stiffly at attention, obedient and trusting, yellow T-shirt taut over his chubbiness, his smile a joyless, obliging curve. I feel such a rush of love and sadness I can hardly bear it – I want to run over to him and crush him to me and tell him what a magnificent father he has and how everything will be alright. Cinzia is bustling us on.

When we arrive at Gianfranco's apartment, I have a moment of fear. He is not expecting this visit – how will he react? I imagine him asleep, mid-afternoon television turned low in his bedroom. Then we are in the cool building and he is standing at the front door in his dressing gown ushering in Tonino with exclamations of pleasure. Cinzia hovers uncertainly. I step inside, feeling obscurely embarrassed. And then there is Nadia stepping out of Gianfranco's bedroom clutching her cigarettes and lighter and looking shy and sheepish. In the sanctuary of my room I hear Gianfranco introduce her to his son and, later, on my way out, I glimpse the three of them on his bed with the television on too loudly.

Mangiare senza bere è come
il tuono senza pioggia
Eating without drinking is like
thunder without rain

My days are running out. I feel I have barely seen, rarely spoken properly, with Gianfranco. The very expensive bottle of Chianti he showed me the day I arrived, with the promise that we would get gloriously drunk on it together, is still on its shelf in the kitchen of his apartment, alongside the white wine I brought him from Australia. We had that drive into the Metro and the conversation about the Italian dinner parties that I should start holding upon my return to Australia to rescue me from debt, but we have not stood side by side in the restaurant's cavernous kitchen while he has cooked and explained, and I have learned.

There were times I was reminded of the precious quality of the man. Gushing to him about how beautifully everything is done in Italy, I became aware that he was smiling at me.

'It is vanity,' he explained. 'It's because Italians are so vain that they seek to do everything as perfectly as possible – it is impelled by vanity.'

During our regular lunches at Nello, I have had more time and conversation with Paolo and Silvana. I recognise how busy Gianfranco is and how much he has on his mind, but I see, too, that it is because of Nadia that there has been no time for me. He stands impatiently in the hallway in the mornings waiting for her to emerge from a bathroom she has strewn with a surprisingly large assortment of cosmetics and creams. I think, 'How brave of you, Nadia,' remembering how conscious I was, years ago, to intrude as little as possible on Gianfranco's life, to behave irreproachably, neatly, beautifully. Her tiny G-strings flutter from the clothesline on the balcony, her footwear lines up alongside her lover's. One day I notice that the bathroom has been scoured, scrubbed and disinfected, and I recognise the work of a woman.

Silvana and I discuss how long it will be before he tires of her. There is a rare evening when we are at a table together and I am struck by a look of such sullen, peasant poutishness on Nadia's face that a headscarf materialising suddenly would not have surprised me. Yet presumably something is working, despite Gianfranco's look of customary ill humour.

The night when Giorgio drops me off after dinner at Artimino, I let myself into the apartment and come face to face with Nadia, looking wretched.

'How are you?' I ask gently.

'He's not speaking to me!' she whispers, and my nastiness drops away at once. I feel like saying to her, 'Leave this man; he will never make you happy – this is what he does, this unspeakable ostracism. Leave before you become even more attached.' Instead, I smile soothingly and tell her not to worry, that he is a moody man and will snap out of it soon. I could not save her, even if I were a better person.

Aiutati che Dio ti aiuta
God helps those that help themselves

Ignazio meets me at Beppe's bar, clicking briskly across the cobbled square in a wide-legged suit shot with silk. He looks beautiful, miniature, and I am feeling gorgeous in tight white flares and my new pink floral jacket. My last night in Tuscany and we are going to dinner together at La Tenda Rossa. We have spent a little more time together, perhaps, than have Gianfranco and I, but this is our first 'date', an attempt the previous week by Ignazio for me to meet his five-year-old daughter having failed when we both decided the arrangement was too logistically complicated.

The entrance is disappointing – it is a low building like a motel. We enter a hushed room filled with palms and vast vases of flowers and a Korean waiter glides out of the shadows to conduct us to our table in the dining room; each immaculately set table has a piece of sculpture laid across it. There are only two other couples dining, but I am noticing the Liberty print stool between our chairs, the exquisite napkin holder and the silver under-plates. The waiter brings us tall, stiff menus (mine, naturally, without the prices) and returns to splash out translucent prosecco into our glasses. A gracious footnote on the menu begs the extremely valuable guest to bear with the possibility of a delay, which may seem long but is because *'noi cuciniamo solo per Lei'* – we are cooking for you personally.

I order cream of asparagus with scallops and Ignazio the duck pâté. Six seared molluscs arrive in a puddle of bright green, their faint smokiness bleeding into the delicacy of the asparagus. Ignazio's rich and buttery pâté arrives accompanied by a neat prism of berry-flavoured jelly and a tiny glass of Sauternes. Classical piano ripples through the room and the three waiters flit soundlessly, administering to the six diners.

Ignazio and I are arguing about Florence in undertones, and then moving onto the subject of his daughter. I bring up my abortion, willing him to tell me that I was the love of his life, but instead he is restrained, as stuffy as this formal setting, as if dictated by it. I feel like shouting, drinking too much, snapping my fingers, but behave beautifully. This is, after all, his treat.

My pigeon arrives in a sticky pool of port, ineffably tender meat falling apart on a pillow of cloudy polenta. Ignazio's lamb medallions are scented with chestnut honey, and we are sipping a mellow Percarlo red in our candle-lit corner. When he slips outside for a cigarette, I jot in my notebook about the stuffy and overblown nature of the restaurant and decide that, despite the gorgeous flavours on our plates, such modern, clever food in a contemporary setting is what Italian restaurateurs manage less well than they do peasant and traditional. It lacks the sublime old character I love so much. When Ignazio returns, we share a delicate soufflé of Brie in a swirl of honey chunked with caramelised apple and crunchy walnuts, and I agree we need more alcohol. So after he has paid the formidable bill (discreetly out the front as I finish my dessert wine), we head off in his car looking for an open bar.

The only one we find is in the Piazza Beccaria and we sit with margaritas at a dim, sticky table and, finally, we begin to talk. We talk about the couple we once were, and the relationship we once had, and I see Ignazio's eyes glitter with tears. He is telling me the loveliest things I only ever dared to dream he might, and in doing so he seems somehow to be validating that period in our lives and making it sacred. In the car afterwards, he turns to me suddenly, halted at traffic lights, and covers my mouth with his perfectly formed Cupid's lips, then whispers in my ear what a shame it was we had not stayed together, what a shame we did not last. The sweet ease of closure I feel spring up inside me has finally come – eighteen years later, but it is there.

Silvana, whose birthday it is, is gloomy about her weight, so in the cool interior of Nello, on my last day, orders crostini with prosciutto followed by meat simmered in broth and spinach. I feel appalling. I have barely slept, my head faintly ringing and stomach uneasy. At Silvana's insistence, I order *panzanella* and grilled porcini; Paolo chooses a veal chop.

At Gianfranco's flat that morning, I had discovered to my horror a complete absence of water. I washed myself ineptly with three bottles of mineral water but still feel, sitting beside gleaming, glowing Silvana and neat, elegant Paolo, as if the previous evening's rich food, dessert wines and cocktails are somehow seeping through my flesh.

My *panzanella* (bread salad) strewn with fresh basil leaves is like eating mouthfuls of summer, but halfway through the porcini, charred and a little smoky on the outside, I am struck by nausea. Our conversation lacks its usual gossipy, trivial exuberance. Paolo eats quickly and seems less expansive than usual, and I have begun to worry about missing my Florence to Perugia train.

Outside the restaurant we hug each other affectionately, and then with long strides I am covering the downhill streets that lead to the villa. It is as if summer has begun. In the big kitchen, one chef is stuffing suckling pig, while the other is showing Nadia how to clean artichokes. I sit out in the little courtyard on the stone wall looking in, waiting for Ignazio, who has offered to drive me to the station in Florence. Nadia has a long white apron bound around her slender waist and seems quite comfortable at the chopping board, her fingers snapping outer layers of artichoke with confidence. I wryly muse if her love affair and resulting culinary apprenticeship will transform her life the way it did mine. I wish her luck, first silently and then into her ear when I say goodbye.

Back at Gianfranco's apartment, Ignazio and I are loading my luggage into his car – my too-much luggage; how could it have expanded so much? – when a four-wheel drive squeals to a halt beside us. Gianfranco has driven back to say farewell to me and, in spite of Nadia's face through the darkened windscreen, I lean closely into him, firmly encircle him with my arms, thank him for his hospitality and friendship, murmur regrets about how little I saw of him.

'Ring me from Perugia,' he urges, and I promise to do so. Then Ignazio and I drive away through the curves and loops of the Chianti countryside, heading to Florence.

Bacco, tabacco e Venere
riducono l'uomo in cenere
Wine, women and tobacco can ruin a man

If it had been fifty years separating our last encounter, I still would have recognised Raimondo. I know only one person who walks in this particular way – quickly, with short steps and solid purpose, heeled boots tapping – and only one person who, impervious to seasons and fashions, wears a suit and a tie. Today the cravat is bright-red silk with a matching pocket handkerchief, a jacket and the signature moustache even more cartoon-like than ever. We fly towards each other at the entrance to the station, exclaiming over each other's youth and beauty. In fact, sitting beside Raimondo in his little Fiat I can see that he has aged, though handsomely. He is thicker-waisted and grey-haired, and I calculate that he must be over sixty now.

Negotiating the vehicle up the curling hill road that leads to town, he is talking about his restaurant, his ever-increasing popularity, and finally his problematic adolescent son. We have too much to tell each other, and each bend we turn through a medieval town is almost as conducive to nostalgia as Florence. I am now hearing about Natasha, Raimondo's Ukrainian girlfriend. He is treating the subject with caution because, even though it is eight years since our beloved Annamaria died, he is aware of the depth of our friendship. Raimondo punctuates our conversation with bursts of song and toots of horn and invective against every inept driver on the road, and miraculously finds a spot to park within minutes of narrow Via Ulisse Rocchi and his restaurant.

Vecchia Perusia is unchanged. There is still the gracious antipasto table forming the centrepiece of one small room, still the pale prettiness of Franca, the chef, through the kitchen pass. A giant woman greets us – the famous Natasha – her eyes flicking swiftly over me and her handshake restrained, then Raimondo is drawing me into the tiny washing-up space behind the kitchen and slopping white wine into two glasses. We toast each other and drink. Raimondo is doing the same thing with his eyes that he always did around Annamaria, a her-against-us look like some naughty schoolboy, and we laugh together in cosy complicity.

I had never lived or stayed long enough in Perugia to cultivate friends; Raimondo is the only person I know. With so little time here, I am content just to roam and drift in the same unstructured semi-purposeless way I did in Florence. I am staying at Annamaria's apartment in town, sharing space with Natasha and Lidia, a surly Latvian teenager who is the restaurant dishwasher. Raimondo commutes between town and the *casa colonica* on the outskirts where he lives with his difficult son. Natasha sits at the kitchen table swathed in a masculine dressing gown, sipping tea and explaining to me how the washing machine works – almost palpably, I feel the memory of Annamaria and me drinking and talking and laughing at the same table. I miss her shockingly.

Later on that first day I shower and dress and walk to the restaurant. Raimondo seats me at a table near the entrance, brings me wine, urges me to help myself to anything off the menu, sits with me and drinks. There are not many customers and Natasha is orchestrating everything smoothly, with occasional darting glances towards our table.

I love Raimondo's restaurant. If ever I were mad enough to consider a return to the ruthless, unforgiving world of restaurants, I could do it in this one. Its intimate smallness, the radio audible from the kitchen where glamorous, plump Franca reigns, Franca whose lips are carefully outlined with dark lipliner. Eight green-clothed tables, each with little vases of fresh flowers. There are the photographs in frames around the walls of Raimondo: Raimondo and his boxer friend Gian Carlo, Raimondo on national television, Raimondo arms around smiling customers. And the refrigerated cabinet with its little pots of tiramisu and glass bowl of fresh strawberries in a glaze of sugar and lemon. The antipasto table with vegetables prepared ten different ways, half a sweet pecorino cheese, fresh fruit salad. The prosciutto stand with its haunch of moist rosy ham, the bread board, a litter of crumbs and chunks of irresistible chewy breads.

Raimondo tells me about the ulcer he has nursed for much of his adult life with periodic abstention from alcohol and drinking lots of milk. He had doubled the dose of his tablets for my visit in order that he and I can be as excessive as we generally are together. At six o'clock every morning, he is saying, he is prowling around his vegetable garden with a beer, gathering the produce to bring to the restaurant. Tough peasant stock has produced this extraordinary man who, well into his sixties, is now discussing the inexhaustible sex that he and Natasha enjoy; privately, I worry for him.

I walk, eat and drink. Lunchtimes, I am usually in the restaurant eating salad from Raimondo's garden, well dressed and accompanied by springy, crunchy bread and several glasses of house white wine diluted with sparkling mineral water, and then it's back out into the sunshine, the shops and piazzas and people-watching, the cafés and steep-stepped streets leading to cool cul-de-sacs, Etruscan ruins, the sudden dizzy panorama of fields folding and falling away below. Back, eventually, ordering dinner. Franca sends out bowls of eggy tagliatelle with fat creamy broad beans and pancetta; or thick tubular *stringozzi* glistening with butter and black truffles; or a plate of garlicky artichoke hearts swimming in oil. I am not caring any more about weight and greed. This sort of gorgeous, big-flavoured food will only ever taste this way here, and I want to trap the memory of it somehow.

BOOK FOUR

Franca and I have been discussing men, middle age, sex, love and death, standing in the tiny kitchen where she keeps half an eye on the simmering sauces. I have had to leave my table to tell her how extraordinary the rabbit *cacciatore* was. How does she manage the intensity of flavours – that jammy, sticky, herbaceous sauce? Talking with passion about food leads us everywhere else, and inevitably to her familiar refrain about long, hard and often thankless hours and the desirability of retirement.

Standing opposite her I am conscious of the urge to grab a wooden spoon to stir or a knife to chop. I have, above all, a wild desire to take over the kitchen, to stay for ever in Italy, to cook and live simply.

Three and a half weeks is all it has taken to diminish my Australian life to an insignificance I am suddenly prepared to abandon. How could I have stayed away from Italy for so long? How could I leave this country again? It is as if the food is just a symbol, an expression of everything that inspires, animates and activates a part of me that ceases to exist when I leave. As if I am two people, or simply a more complete woman. An outer layering, perhaps, which thickens and enriches my entire being, turning me into something else again – the same, though better. It is a sensation encountered whenever I am re-immersed in Italy but which only now I am capable of articulating and understanding. 'Retire', I feel like saying to Franca, 'and your kitchen will be safe in my capable hands.'

When Natasha is convinced that I have no designs on Raimondo – assisted by a little lecture he later tells me he delivered to her – her iciness drops away. We are just two foreign women in Italy, and she is as eager to take me shopping as Silvana had been. Yet, whereas my expeditions with Silvana whirled me through emporia whose flimsy fantasy garments I could only ever dream of affording, Natasha's take me to bargain basements and cut-price boutiques for teenage girls with thumping stereos and tables piled high with cheap, bright clothing. This is a side of elegant Perugia I never knew and, while she selects garments for a twenty-three-year-old daughter she never sees, I am trying on endless pairs of jeans and shirts whose prices are laughable.

We browse through a dreary downmarket department store, where, bored, I wait for Natasha to finish a long conversation in Russian with another couple, then attempt to persuade me to buy kitschy knick-knacks as coming-home gifts for my family and friends. We end up in one of the town's more beautiful pastry shops, where Natasha orders a spectacularly fattening cream cake. She tells me she will soon be starting a regime of strict exercise. How I love women!

Back at the restaurant, I see how invaluable Natasha is to my beloved crazy Raimondo, and how much of the business she takes care of. She sets up the theatre for his performances, enabling him to flourish in his various alter egos, to slip away and do the round of Perugia bars in quieter moments, to drink too much and sing too loudly to his customers.

I have always understood Raimondo. Incomprehensible to me is how I have managed to listen to his mix of Umbrian, Romagnol and alcohol, and understand nearly everything he is saying. If I believed in past lives I would say that he and I belonged as siblings to some other time. I remain his *sorellina*, the little sister he takes on his prowls around town, one arm through mine. Wherever we go we are greeted with enthusiasm. Raimondo is a celebrity, a character more colourful than most others, and I am proud to be with him.

At the sumptuously elegant Caffè del Perugia he is conversing with the maître d'. We balance Campari cocktails and I am spellbound by the food. All along the S-shaped bar and on tabletops are platters of antipasti, tiny little *pizzette*, sandwiches, marinated vegetables, cheeses, dips and terrines and meats, miniature stuffed rolls, olives, crostini and bruschetta, bowls of pistachios and almonds and peanuts, and the exquisitely dressed crowd of Perugians is helping itself with that unselfconscious, graceful indifference Italians display when they eat.

An elderly man in a creased cream linen suit has joined our little group and Raimondo introduces him as the owner, explaining simultaneously that I am a famous Australian journalist. Raimondo's expansion of the truth is one of his hallmarks and I play along, allowing myself to be swept into a lift and whisked up to the next level of the building, where there is a formal restaurant under a vaulted ceiling of chandeliers. I ask intelligent questions, admire the open kitchen where a file of beautiful chefs in blinding white troops out to meet me, run my hands over the marble and terracotta, study menus, gush with suitable rapture. My heart turns with sadness in the lift going down, when I notice the hearing aids in the owner's ears, which he adjusts from time to time. I thank him graciously and go to find Raimondo.

As we walk back to his restaurant he tells me about his son, his greatest sorrow. He fears that Riccardo has been involved in drugs. Whatever happened has resulted in behaviour bizarre and antisocial, a boy in his room all day, screaming arguments between father and son, and a need for professional intervention. During one fight, which became physical, Raimondo relates, he pretended that Riccardo had knocked him out and he lay on the ground as if dead. He let Riccardo's mortification drag on for as long as he could before 'coming to', as if to discover whether his son really loved him.

Riccardo would have been thirteen when Annamaria died, and I still remember how close they were to each other in that special way I have observed in older mothers and their only sons. How did a hard-drinking, heavy-smoking restaurateur manage, then, on his own? I am utterly sad to hear Raimondo's story, and helpless in my attempts at advice, yet privately unsurprised. We have arrived at Vecchia Perusia and Raimondo's brief moment of tears is replaced by the rousing welcome in three languages he bellows as we enter. Natasha's smile is pure relief.

Questa è la vita e qui il gioire,
un'ora di abbracci e poi moire
This is life and this is joy, an hour
of embracing and then to die

I have pressed as much as possible into my suitcases. Languid rain drips from my umbrella as I clip up the steep cobbled streets leading to Vecchia Perusia for my last night in Perugia. An early train will bear me away to Rome in the morning and the long haul back to Australia. Only two tables are occupied in the restaurant. It is a Sunday and Raimondo has planned to take me for a final drink. I eat my last solemn supper of tiny Brussels sprouts, fennel, artichoke and chargrilled zucchini in a pool of fragrant oil I blot up with bread, then a wedge of Franca's gorgeous ricotta tart with its buttery short pastry and chunks of chocolate and mysterious indefinable spices. I take photos of her framed by the window, of Natasha putting her hands up in horror or modesty, of Raimondo standing before the antipasti table, then of Raimondo and Natasha and the strawberry cheesecake I made the previous afternoon.

Then he and I are wheeling arm in arm out into the damp, soft night. An African materialises with roses and Raimondo buys me one. Then a car slowly passes and its owner winds down the window to invite us to a party in a nearby restaurant. First, we clatter down steps and through a low-roofed doorway into a noisy trattoria where glasses of limoncello are poured for us at the bar, then into another bar for cocktails, surrounded by waiters who joke with Raimondo and recount anecdotes. The party we eventually reach is, apparently, for a visiting American, to whom I am briefly introduced, the room full of fashionable, expensive people who are sitting around a long table.

Flutes of champagne are poured for Raimondo and me and I am transfixed, as usual, by the display of food, entire smoked salmons and a glittering jewel-like array of antipasti and baskets of breads and rolls and whole cheeses. Wishing

I were hungry, wishing I were never leaving. Wishing I were one of these glamorous, beautiful Perugians for whom such opulence is casual and regular. Feeling so proud of Raimondo, feeling scruffily, ploddingly Australian, for all my newly discovered layers.

I had encircled Raimondo's neck from behind, rested my head briefly on top of his and said a casual goodnight, leaving him at the table with Natasha as I climbed up to bed. This was the only farewell he would accept from me. And so the following morning it is Natasha who is waiting for the taxi with me at the bottom of the street. Perugia is still sleeping and a mist of fine white cloud hangs over folds of fields beyond the town's fortifications. I have slept little and badly, mentally rehearsing the taxi to the station, the train to Rome, then the train to the airport, the checking-in followed by the long flight home.

It seems easier to stay – and yet I am suddenly anxious to be gone, to be occupying that strange, surreal, limbo-like state of travel in order to absorb the past weeks. When the train rolls smoothly out of Perugia, I feel fragile with emotion, but I am also beginning to consider what lies ahead: a job I enjoy, a beautiful place to live, a man who makes me happy. I am seeing how all the disparate elements and adventures of my past have brought me there and somehow enmeshed to form the richly textured medium in which I move, and the person I now am.

Index of Recipes

INDEX OF RECIPES

About the Author

Victoria Cosford completed a Bachelor of Arts degree in languages, including Italian, and has taught Italian cooking for over twenty years. Since 2002 Victoria has lived in Byron Bay, Australia and written a popular weekly food column for local newspaper the *Byron Shire Echo*, where she is employed as a journalist.

Have you enjoyed this book? If so, why not write a review
on your favourite website?

Thanks very much for buying this McArthur & Company book.

www.mcarthur-co.com